THE STRANGER IN READING

The Stranger
in
READING

JOHN MAN

edited by Adam Sowan

illustrated by Andy Clarke

TWO RIVERS PRESS

Published in the UK in 2005 by Two Rivers Press
35–39 London Street, Reading RG1 4PS
www.tworiverspress.com

Introduction and notes © Adam Sowan
Cover image and new illustrations © Andy Clarke

ISBN 1-901677-44-3
978-1-901677-44-7

The publisher acknowledges financial assistance
from the Arts Council of England

Printed and bound by CPI Bath
on 130gsm off-white cartridge

Designed and typeset by Rob Banham using
Monotype Bulmer and Berthold Akzidenz Grotesk

ACKNOWLEDGEMENTS

I would like to thank the following for their help with this project: David Man for permission to quote from his genealogical website; Barbara Morris for transcribing John Man's typographically challenging text; Sidney Gold, Reg Martin and Paul Sowan for advice in their respective fields of expertise; and the staff of Reading Local Studies Library and Berkshire Record Office for their usual helpfulness and efficiency.

Other books by Adam Sowan

The Holy Brook

A Much-Maligned Town: Opinions of Reading 1586–1997

Abattoirs Road to Zinzan Street

CONTENTS

PREFACE

The Stranger in Reading is a lively and idiosyncratic account of the town, published anonymously in 1810; the author, a retired schoolmaster, pretended to be an outsider. I first encountered it while collecting material for *A Much-Maligned Town,* an anthology of opinions of Reading over the last four centuries; Man provided me with some irresistible passages, largely because he was the first commentator to give the town anything resembling a bad press. As I re-read the book and learnt more about its author, I began to feel a strong affinity with John Man. Like him, I was born in London but have lived in Reading for 30 years and more; I too retired early from full-time work, and am now about the same age as he was when he wrote the *Stranger*; I share his affection for the town and also his exasperation at its shortcomings; I also collect books, and have myself written several about Reading. As the *Stranger* approaches its bicentenary it seems to me that this significant and entertaining book deserves a wider circulation, joining several other reprinted accounts of a town that was just starting to expand and change radically, with marketing giving way to manufacturing.

I have silently corrected a few obvious typos in Man's text, but otherwise it is reproduced verbatim, with his spelling and his liberal use of capitals and italics. His generous punctuation remains intact (one sentence contains three colons, five semicolons and no fewer than thirty-two commas;

yet it is surprisingly readable). Man's title-page, three original illustrations, and a sample page layout appear in facsimile between pp.128–132. His footnotes retain their place under his text, while my own comments and clarifications are set alongside. The subheadings summarising the contents of each letter are mine.

INTRODUCTION

The Family of Man

There had been Mans in the environs of Reading long before
the author of this book came to live and work in the town in
the late 18th century. The earliest so far traced was Jonas Man,
born in 1596 in Hambleden, Bucks; his descendants crossed
the Thames to Wargrave, where the Stranger's grandfather
(John I) was a joiner. He later moved to Hurst, where he was
living in some comfort until his death in 1750. His son (John
II, 1718–83) was an architect/builder in Whitechapel, London, moving to Croydon in 1756. In the 1760s he got into debt
and deliberately disappeared, resurfacing in Wales under the
name of Thomas Roberts and resuming his old trade. John
III – the Stranger – last saw his father in Knighton in 1769; a
further attempt to make contact in 1787 took him to Cardiff,
but he was four years too late. John II's former landlady said
'there was never a better man on earth'; he was 'sober, honest, quiet, humane, good natured…' and 'reckoned a very in-
genious architect'. John III was deeply affected by this trip; a
letter to his brother James ends 'This life has few comforts for
me… May God forgive us'. There are hints of family feuds,
and John II's wife seems to have been a difficult and disagree-
able person. James was an importer of rum and other com-
modities; he died in 1823.

John III's other brother Henry (1747–99) worked for the
South Sea Company alongside Charles Lamb, and was also

a writer; he is noted in the *Dictionary of National Biography*. In January 1800 the *Reading Mercury* published (probably at John's instigation) a poem 'by the late Henry Man, of facetious memory'. John also had four sisters. Mary died in infancy; the other three all came to Reading. Ann, born in 1753, was blind, and died unmarried at Southampton Street in 1831; Frances (Fanny), born in 57, also remained a spinster, and died at Coley Place in 1842; Mariah, born in 60, married James Taylor (who had taken over John's school) in 1796, but died, possibly in childbirth, the following year.

The Man John

John Man III, the Stranger, is now mainly known as Reading's second historian. His very name sounds like a pseudonym – John Doe meets Everyman, perhaps – but he was real enough; what we know of him comes from his published and unpublished writings, occasional mentions and adverts in the *Mercury,* a very helpful website charting the family's history, and a few other sources listed in the bibliography. He was born and baptised in Whitechapel in 1749, when his parents were living in Mansell Street, just outside the City of London. John was almost certainly educated alongside his brother Henry by the Rev. John Lamb at Whitgift School in Croydon. This is now a large and prestigious establishment, but in the 1760s it was in decline; its historian F H G Percy describes it as 'a small school for unambitious pupils'. His brother Henry's *DNB* entry refers to a 'nonconformist background' which prevented him from entering a university; we know nothing more of young John's life until he moved to Reading.

He arrived in 1770, and at some time within the next five years was appointed assistant master at William Baker's Academy in Hosier's Lane, north of Castle Street. This may well have been in 1773, when Baker felt obliged to publicly deny a rumour that he was about to retire. The introduction was possibly made by Henry Man, who was working in the City near Baker's son, also William; the latter is mentioned in the *Stranger's* Letter 4, and achieved sufficient fame as a printer to merit an entry in the *DNB*. In 1775 John married Baker's daughter Sarah – his senior by nine years – and acquired a half share in the school. The couple soon had four children: Henry was born in 1776, William in 78, Anna Maria in 80 and Horace in 82. (Horace's name may have been inspired by Sir Horace Mann – no relation – who in 1782 advocated a government of national unity; he was also an early devotee of cricket, and had played in Berkshire. This may be a clue to John's opinions and interests.)

School Man

When Baker did retire, in 1779, he put a notice in the *Mercury* in which he 'begs leave to recommend Mr Man as every way qualified to succeed him', and it is from Man's teaching career that we learn most about his character. In the late 18th century – and indeed until 1870 – no child was obliged to undergo any formal schooling. J M Guilding estimated that in 1812 some 900 children went to school when the population was about 11,000. The sons of the rich could go to Eton, Harrow and the like, which were taking custom away from local grammars such as Reading School (which was still officially 'free', but effectively charged fees). The poor had to rely on an assortment of charitable institutions; from Man's *History* we learn that in 1809 there was one for boys, one mixed, and two for girls; one of these last he chides for being little more than a sweatshop producing cheap needlework. But times were changing fast: within two years both the Christian National (mixed) and the Lancastrian or British Schools (boys) had opened.

Between these extremes, the moderately well-off had a widening choice of private academies such as Man's; most were single-sex, and boys of course fared better than girls. Baker had run his school since about 1740; Coates, in his *History*, describes him as 'a man of amiable character and manners, of great classical and mathematical learning'. In 1773 he was boarding young gentlemen and teaching them writing, arithmetic, mathematics, Latin and Greek; young ladies had to be content with writing and 'accompts' – i.e. household accounts. By the time Man took over, girls are no longer mentioned; the boys could also learn French, Italian, merchants' accounts, the use of the globes, and 'natural shorthand'; a few months later he added 'every branch of useful and polite literature' and 'dancing and drawing by the best masters'. Navigation joined the curriculum in 1782, and in 1786 he promises 'mensuration in its various kinds', geometry, trigonometry and geography; he stresses the importance of French since the signing of a new commercial treaty. His fees were 16 guineas a year; these, and the range of subjects offered, were very similar to other local schools. After his retirement, when he was seeking a new tenant-schoolmaster in 1799, he boasted that 'the house has been built within a very few years for the express purpose of a Boarding School, and has every accommodation for 40 pupils, with a good kitchen garden, and spacious play-ground walled in…'.

As well as Baker's recommendation we have two or three other clues to what sort of schoolmaster – and man – Man was. In January 1782 the *Mercury* printed a letter from 'An Advocate for a Liberal Education' condemning corporal punishment in schools. This could have been written by anybody, but it followed four consecutive weeks' adverts for Man's school; and later that year he was seeking an English assistant 'whose natural disposition will lead him to treat the young gentlemen with good nature, affability and affection'.

That Man himself embraced this ethos is evident from a pupil's-eye view to be found in *Reminiscences of a Literary Life* (1836) by Thomas Frognall Dibdin (1776–1847), nephew of the composer Charles Dibdin. His memories of the school date from his fifth to eleventh years (c.1781–87) when, as an orphan, he was sent to live with a great-aunt in Reading. With hindsight he was glad to have escaped Richard Valpy's regime at Reading School; instead he joined Man's 'small establishment' in 'an obscure part of the town' on 'proportionately moderate terms'. Dibdin paints an affectionate picture of his mentor: 'He was a singular, naturally clever, and kind-hearted man: had a mechanical turn; and could construct electrifying apparatuses, and carve a picture frame.' (In 1778 a Mr Banks, 'experimental philosopher', was touring locally with scientific lectures and demonstrations featuring electricity. The Museum of the History of Science in Oxford has a number of 'electrifying apparatuses' dating from 1786; they were 'popular with amateurs'.) Dibdin continues: 'His studio, of this description, was at the top of the house; and many an hour do I remember to have spent therein, gazing with surprise and delight upon the mysteries of turning, planing and chisselling.' The young Dibdin had to share a bed with John's son Henry; he looked weak and emaciated, and tells us that 'Mr and Mrs Man's unremitting attention and kindness perhaps saved my life'. He was allowed to go into Man's private room whenever he pleased. 'It was sufficiently well filled with books ... *here*, for the first time, I caught, or fancied I caught, the electric spark of the BIBLIOMANIA. My master was now and then the purchaser of old books by the *sack-full*; these were tumbled out upon the floor, the arm-chair, or a table, just as it might happen.' Dibdin was also welcome in old Mr Baker's study. His 'rapturous days' at Reading included bathing in the Holy Brook at the Old Orchard, Coley Park. He says that by the time he left he had made 'little progress in anything but writing, arithmetic and French', but in no way blames Man for a defective education. He went on to become librarian to Lord Spencer, and among his own publications was indeed a volume entitled *Bibliomania.*

Barge Man

In the summer of 1795 Man retired, let the school to James Taylor, and moved to the High Street. He was only 45, and by no means idle: very soon he was Secretary of the Reading Provident Society, and within two years had embarked on a new venture in the growing business of waterborne transport.

The 54 years of Man's residence in Reading span the great age of canal and river navigation. The middle Thames had been much improved by the building of eight new locks in 1772/3, and further enhancements were prompted by the threat of rival canals in the 'mania' of the 1790s. On 6 March 1797 'The Committee appointed to carry into execution the plan of a constant and regular Navigation between Reading and London, beg leave to inform the Public, that a Barge will lie at Mr Blandy's Wharf [by the High Bridge] on Thursday next, to take in loading for London. Orders are received at the Counting-House in the Wharf, or at Mr Man's…'. Man's partner was William Blandy, of the well-known local family, an ironmonger and coal merchant; the enterprise evidently became the Reading Navigation Company, which was still trading in 1800 with Man as Secretary. Man's poem 'The Counting House' in the *Anecdotes* gives us a playful account of a day in the carrying business: the clerk starts very early, checking the barge and warehouses and opening the office; Man arrives later, and after lunch sends out for beer and tobacco from the Lower Ship Inn. Staff and clients relax, 'laughing, drinking, smoking, prating'; the air grows thick, and one of the party peers through the gloom:

'What thing is that I see,
Perch'd like a shuffle in a tree;
Or rather, like a candle snuff,
When just extinguish'd by a puff?
So meagre, sorrowful, and lean…'

The mystery object proves to be Man himself, and this is the only clue we have to his appearance; but the joke may have been that he was actually portly… 'shuffle-wing' was an old and apt nickname for the dunnock or hedge-sparrow.

In April 1802 the 'New Canal' shown on the *Stranger's* map – the 500-metre short cut passing under Watlington Street and the King's Road – was opened, and the *Mercury* tells us that 'a barge freighted from London, belonging to the Navigation Company, on board of which was a great number of respectable inhabitants of this town, sailed up it. There was a blue flag and a laurel bough hoisted at the mast head, and the men were decorated with blue ribbons; she sailed to her moorings amidst a grand discharge of cannon … Afterwards the Navigation Company dined together in their office, where the day was spent with the utmost festivity and hilarity'. In July 1804 the company asked for its sacks to be returned and encouraged debtors and creditors to settle up; it is not clear whether the business was folding. Man certainly retained an interest in water transport until at least 1811, when he was a signatory to a notice calling a meeting of 'noblemen, gentlemen and other friends to the Thames Navigation'; they were concerned at the competition threatened by the many proposals for new canals. A list of Reading barge-owners in 1812 includes Blandy but not Man. Blandy became an alderman and mayor, and worked for the good of the town: he repaired Caversham Bridge and campaigned for the preservation of the Forbury as a public space.

Pen Man

The idea of writing about his adopted town had already been in Man's mind before he retired: he had for some time been collecting material for the *Anecdotes* and the *History* (see below). 1798 saw his first publication: a plan of Reading 'trigonometrically surveyed and carefully delineated, engraved by W Poole and dedicated to the Worshipful the Mayor, Aldermen and Burgesses'. The lack of early maps is a constant disappointment to local historians: Reading's first surviving plan is Speed's of 1610, followed by an anonymous sketch-map of the Civil War defences in 1643. Rocque (1761) and Pride (1790) covered a wider area and have little detail of the town. Man's pioneering effort used a bigger scale than any of these, but was soon eclipsed by the more accurate one by Tomkins, drawn for Coates's *History* of 1802. In a corner of his map Man includes a note giving his estimate of the town's population at 8350 (he was not far out: the first census in 1801 counted 9421).

In 1807 Man's son William joined Robert Snare's printing and bookselling business. The partnership produced a mixture of works, notably including things that might have displeased a less tolerant father: a supplement to Coates's rival *History*; some verses by J B Monck upon the opening of the Literary Institution, rival to the Permanent Library (see below); and psalms and hymns edited by Henry Gauntlett, who (as we shall see) had taken exception to the *Stranger*. In 1816 William left Snare and set up on his own in Broad Street, but he printed very little more. At the age of 83 he married a 22-year-old on the Isle of Wight and fathered a daughter; he died in 1874.

John's wife Sarah died in May 1809. Details of their son Henry's life are a little perplexing. In 1793 – when he was only 16 – Henry Man of Castle Street advertised himself as an importer of foreign spiritous liquors. In December 1797, according to John's *Anecdotes,* 'Harry the lad, who's seldom sad' supplied the beer for the family's New Year party. By 1808 he had progressed to London, and was married (by his old schoolfellow and bedfellow Thomas Dibdin) to Mrs Dennett, a widow with a small family. Dibdin says he died in 1810, but there are later extant letters; he clearly did not outlive his father, as he is not mentioned in John's Will.

Both John and Horace were on the committee of the Reading Permanent Library, founded in 1807, which in the event proved decidedly temporary; the rival Literary Institution fared better. In 1809 John, William and Henry were signatories to a request for a meeting on Forbury Hill to discuss 'the propriety of celebrating George III's Jubilee': they objected to Corporation-sponsored fireworks, and asserted 'the right of the people to assemble and express their own sentiments, in their own style, on all public occasions'. (The political journalist William Cobbett made a similar complaint.) By 1810 – the year of the *Stranger* – Man is listed in a Poll Book as a Gentleman, of Castle Street, having apparently moved back from the High Street. In 1816 he produced his *History,* insisting in his preface that he is 'not an author by profession'.

Horace had taken a steady job as agent for the Globe Fire Office in 1804. He contributed to a fund for the relief of the poor in 1813, but otherwise there is no news until his death in 1817 at the age of 35 in 'a melancholy accident'. He was sailing up to Pangbourne with two friends when they were caught by a strong wind, and the boom knocked him into the Thames. William took over his insurance job.

John Man wrote an account of the churches of Wallingford in 1818; and died, aged 75, on 10 April 1824. A letter from William tells of the end: 'I am sure you will be much grieved to learn of the death of my poor father, who this morning expired after a protracted illness, in great measure occasioned by that most distressing of maladies, the stone, and which he was able to bear up against with a tolerable degree of fortitude to the last moments of his life. The asthma which so much affected him in an early stage of the illness, and which you will recollect, so distressed him when you were last with us, had for some considerable time left him and his general good state of health did not seem to have been in the least impaired by it. Indeed his constitution was so strong as to let him exist a whole fortnight without taking the least sustenance except his medicines, which I understand are soporifics and of which during the last few days of his life he was deprived, not being able to swallow them. My sister who is almost worn out by her increasing attentions to him, and for whose health I have much anxiety joins me in kind love to yourself and family.' The *Mercury* merely noted his death, with no obituary. His Will left two adjacent houses in Castle Street – then numbered 47 & 48, they were demolished to make way for the IDR roundabout – along with six cottages that he had built at the north end of the property, and also some land at Binfield which he had probably inherited. He had already given his books and instruments to William, and his furniture to his daughter Anna Maria; she remained a spinster until her death in 1860 at Jesse Terrace.

The full title is *The Stranger in Reading, in a series of letters, from a traveller, to his friend in London.* The self-conscious use of the word 'stranger' to mean 'one of us, on unfamiliar ground' goes back at least as far as 1754, when *A New Traveller's Companion through the Netherlands* recommended 'things to be taken notice on by a stranger'. The first book to use it in a title was Sir John Carr's *The Stranger in France*, in 1803, followed rapidly by *The Stranger in England, or Travels in Great Britain* (a translation from the German). By 1807 there were *Strangers in* (or *Stranger's Guides to*) Ireland (Carr again), Glasgow, Liverpool, London, and America; these last two were advertised in the *Mercury* in 1808, and may well have given Man the idea for his own title. After Reading the flow eased up, with five more *Strangers* by 1825 and a trickle thereafter.

The Stranger in Reading was printed in 1810 by Robert Snare and William Man, and sold by Snare and others. The unnamed author took some pains to construct a back-story for the 'letters'. Only the first and last are dated, and they imply that the Stranger spent a year in Reading. They are carefully organised, each covering a different topic (although the state of the pavements is a recurring refrain). They have somehow reached the 'editor', who adds a preface (in which Man comments on his own views on Methodists), a dedication, and footnotes. The title-page bears two quotations: the Latin one is from the poet Horace, and means 'What prevents me from telling the truth with a smile?' and the Italian one is the old saying 'In the land of the blind, the one-eyed man is king'.

So the writer is telling us not to take him too seriously, and that he knows his subject better than most. It was clear that the Stranger was entirely familiar with the town, its politics and its religious life; and (as we shall see) it took little time or ingenuity, in a small-town society with few plausible suspects, to nail John Man as the author.

Two further books need to be mentioned. In 1859 George Hillier brought out *The Strangers' Guide to the Town of Reading, with a history of the abbey, a description of the churches, and everything worthy of notice.* Its content is not dissimilar to Man's work, though less entertaining; it is worth a look, if only for the amazing list of relics once claimed by the Abbey. A century later, David Cliffe borrowed Man's title for a slim unofficial guide, again with perambulations. The current reader will be struck by the number of historic buildings which were still under threat as recently as 1978: the Town Hall, the Hospitium, the Turk's Head, St John's Church, and Simonds' Bank.

The Ripostes, and Man Detected

Some of the other early *Stranger* books caused controversy and provoked published ripostes; Carr went so far as to sue one of his critics. Man's effort certainly caused a local stir, prompting two rapid responses, both pseudonymous. *The Stranger in Reading*, price seven shillings, was advertised in the *Mercury* on 29 January 1810; within three weeks, on 19 February, readers were invited to buy *The Compliment Returned to the Stranger in Reading,* by the still unknown 'Philanthropos' ('one who loves mankind'). This advert includes a quotation from the Old Testament Proverbs: 'Answer a Fool according to his Folly/Lest he be wise in his own conceit'. Philanthropos slyly claims to have detected the Stranger's identity when he says 'there is a certain MAN with whom I believe you sometimes converse…'. He points to some factual errors – Man's map puts the Minster Mill on the Holy Brook, and the scale is distorted – but most of his thoughts concern Man's views on religion.

A week later, on 26 February, the *Mercury* promised *A Letter to the Stranger in Reading;* but on 16 April another notice appeared, apologising for the late delivery of what were now to be the plural *Letters,* under the pseudonym 'Detector'. Yet already on 5 March Man had put in another ad, accompanied by a whole column playfully and sarcastically attacking his critics and thanking them for boosting his sales. He refers to Philanthropos, but also to 'the Rev. Detector' (whose counterblast had yet to appear in print) and to 'the other Reverend Gentleman who is announced as a third antagonist of the Stranger, in behalf of the Institute'. This character remains unidentified. Man also disingenuously inserts the tag 'Davos sum, non Oedipus' which Dr Brewer freely renders as 'I am a humble man, and do not understand hints, innuendos and riddles'. Having 'now taken final leave of his opponents' Man claims that his only aim was the improvement of the town, and that he had not intended to offend any individual. The piece is by-lined 'Bath, 26 February', perhaps in a last jocular attempt to hide his identity. Detector's *Letters* finally appeared on 2 July, price five shillings.

Later that month the *Mercury* published two epigrams relating to a separate literary spat between Man and Detector;

they include the lines 'In controversy's listed fields DETECTOR conquers no MAN' and 'He throws the GAUNTLET at them' and 'Brave STRANGER ... is MAN alone by name'. It is clear that the Stranger (Man) and Detector (the Rev. Henry Gauntlett) knew who each other were from the word go, and that the latter took the whole ding-dong rather more seriously than the former.

We know a great deal about Gauntlett (1762–1833) thanks to his daughter Catherine's *Memoir* (1835). He was ordained in the established church and moved around quite a lot in his career, thanks to his strong views and unwillingness to compromise. Before his brief stay in Reading he had already been dismissed from the curacy of Botley, Hants, by a new rector in 1803; and he left Wellington, Salop, because his sentiments on the 17th Article (the one about Predestination and Election) and other points were opposed to the vicar's. He supported the Evangelical Revival, and was attracted to the 'partial conformity' of the relatively new breakaway chapel of St Mary, Castle Street, which was not under episcopal jurisdiction. (See John Dearing's *The Church That Would Not Die* for a full account of its history.) Gauntlett took charge there in August 1805, but in October 1807 returned to the full Anglican fold at Nettlebed and Pishill. He continued to live in Reading until 1811, however, so was well able to observe local life; he founded a Lord's Day Observance Society, which succeeded in banning the driving of cattle through the town on Sundays. He saw theatres as 'nurseries of vice and crime'. His *Letters* start by calling Man's work 'despicable', saying that it 'may have left an unfavourable impression of the Inhabitants of Reading'. He goes on in stronger vein, hiding behind the views of 'a friend' who finds Man 'a sinner against style, fact, and principle ... such works must perish ... he proves himself ... to be an infidel of the very basest sort'. Catherine Gauntlett loyally weighs in, calling the *Stranger* 'a vehicle for mis-stating facts, calumniating individuals, and ridiculing religion'. Its author she characterises as 'an elderly person [Man was 62] of deistical principles, resident in the town'. 'Deist' was for two centuries a pejorative term for one who believed in some kind of God but had no religion; but from Man's comments near the end of Letter 5 he cannot have been such. Catherine goes on to admit that the book 'excited a lively interest in the neighbourhood'; she also claims that John Simeon, Tory MP for Reading 1806–18, agreed with the sentiments in her father's *Letters*. Robin Leaver's history of the Castle Street church claims that Gauntlett effectively prevented Man from publishing his promised 'further volume', i.e. the *Anecdotes* (see below).

The *Stranger,* both of the ripostes, and the *History* are all listed in Snare's 1832 catalogue of some 13,000 items. In 1887 there appeared a book called *Reading Seventy Years Ago,* consisting of edited extracts from a diary from 1813–19; its author, still unknown, confidently ascribes the *Stranger* to John Man – and accuses him of 'a great many errors'. In 1895 J M Guilding wrote *Notable Events in the Municipal History of Reading*; in it he says that the *Stranger* 'contains severe animadversions on the sanitary state and administration of the town'. *The Reading Handbook* for 1906, mentioning accounts of the town, says '...there are Miss Mitford's sunny sketches in 'Belford Regis', and there are the grey shadows thrown by 'The Stranger'. Modern local historians, however, have found it an invaluable primary source for the period.

Were the Stranger's criticisms fair, or was he just a grumpy middle-aged Man? Was his tongue firmly in his cheek? Was Reading worse than other towns of its size, or was he making unreasonable comparisons with London? Did he change Reading for the better? For a different contemporary view of the town we can sample William Fordyce Mavor's *General View of the Agriculture of Berkshire* (1813): he finds it 'delightfully situated', and the houses 'well built and commodious'. He goes on: 'An air of gentility is thrown over the place; and there is an elegant sociability in the manners of the inhabitants, which is irresistibly attractive to strangers.' He concludes '... there is not a country town in the kingdom that unites so many charms and advantages to persons of independent fortune, and cultivated minds. ...[it is] in every respect the first town in Berkshire'.

One of the *Stranger's* most distinctive features is the stream of complaints about the state of the streets – and especially the pavements – that runs through the book; he should perhaps be nominated as a posthumous president of Living Streets (formerly known as the Pedestrians' Association). It is possible that he was severely myopic – his sister's blindness may indicate an inherited sight impairment – but some attempt needs to be made to discover just how bad things were. In April 1770 the *Mercury* carried a letter from 'A Lover of Useful and Elegant Improvements'. He claims to have just arrived in Reading, 'proposing to continue there a few weeks, and indeed with some intention to settle in that town for life ... but to my great astonishment and disgust, I found the streets

so ill-paved and badly lighted that I quitted it in a few days.'
I suspect that this rare example of a letter about local matters
was from Man – who at that date was a real stranger – and
represents a pre-echo of his later preoccupation; and he did
in fact settle in Reading permanently a few months later. The
state of the streets is hardly mentioned in the local press again
until 1783, when the Corporation warned people about encroachments onto the highway, particularly bow windows.
(Each householder was responsible for the section of road
outside his house.)

The *Reading Improvement Act* (commonly referred to as
the Paving Act) was passed in 1785. Its full title was 'An Act
for paving the Footways in the Borough of Reading, in the
County of Berks, for better repairing, cleansing, lighting, and
watching the Streets, Lanes, Passages, and Places in the said
Borough; and for removing Encroachments, Obstructions,
and Annoyances therefrom, and preventing the like for the
future'. The preamble explains why it had become necessary,
using many of the same words, and describes the Streets (etc)
as 'in some Places very incommodious and unsafe for Travellers and Passengers'. These acts were not imposed by Parliament, but resulted from local pressure; they empowered
people to do things, without any obligation; there were no set
standards and no system of inspection. The work was to be
paid for by levying rates and borrowing money.

The Paving Commissioners – over 200 of them, including
the existing unelected Corporation – made an enthusiastic
start. Within a month they had appealed for voluntary con-
tributions and invited tenders (specifying the types of stone
to be used), and on 8 August staged a ceremonial laying of

the first paviour outside the Mayor's house, with bells ringing and colours flying. The following March they sought to raise more money by selling annuities; in June 1787 they paid off some shares, 'the pavement having been completed considerably within the estimate'; a fortnight later they sought to appoint one or more 'scavengers' – who had to attend the principal streets twice a week 'with cart and bell'. In 1789 the inhabitants of Katesgrove asked that the paving taxes be used to pave their patch. Things seem very quiet in 1794, when the Commissioners met merely to appoint new members to replace those who had moved or died. The following year a further Reading Paving Bill was before Parliament, but it did not become law. In 1797 tenders were invited for maintaining 156 street-lamps; they had increased to 214 by 1808. 1799 brought complaints and hints of neglect: the *Mercury* noted that 'lamps in several streets have for many nights been out by 11 pm'; and a week later 'we are desired to give a hint to the scavengers… to remove the numerous large heaps of dirt'. In 1803 the Commissioners were criticised – there was too much rubbish, the scavengers were ineffective, and the lamps poor. In 1806 there was a scavenger for each of the three parishes. In 1809 we read that 'every inhabitant must long have witnessed with regret the shameful state wherein the streets are suffered to remain'.

Some ten months after the *Stranger's* publication the *Mercury* carried the following paragraph: 'We are desired to call the public's attention to the obstructions and dirt, which some persons have lately made a practice of leaving in the streets of the borough, to the great danger and inconvenience of the public. By the Reading Paving Act the following penalties are incurred – ten shillings, by every person leaving any carriage in the street, except whilst loading or unloading [so parking fines go back to 1785!]; driving a wheelbarrow on the footways; throwing dust, dirt, or rubbish, in the streets. Five shillings, by all persons neglecting to sweep the foot-paths before their houses every morning (Sundays excepted) before ten o'clock.' This item may have been prompted by a request from the Paving Commissioners, but one suspects a bit of chivvying from Man. A fortnight later we read of injuries to an eight-year-old boy caused by an obstructive barrow, and of the dangerous and filthy state of Duke Street and London Street.

A rare word of praise for Man comes from William Silver Darter, former Mayor, in his *Reminiscences of Reading* (1888). In it he recalls that 'about the year 1813, London Street was newly paved with York stone, a work at that time much needed, and the execution of which was accelerated by the severe criticism of the 'Stranger'.' Mavor, quoted above, says 'the streets are spaciously and handsomely paved'. Man himself, in his 1816 *History*, says: 'Under the powers granted by the [1785 Act] the town has been much improved; the streets are well paved and clean, the fronts of the houses better arranged, and every part well lit…'. Some streets were re-paved in 1818, and gas lighting was being considered. Yet in 1823 the Mercury carried more complaints: 'There is no town in England where there was less attention paid to keeping the streets clean, in good order, and passable to traffic'. The truth was, perhaps, that the actual paving and lighting were reasonably well done, but the Commissioners were less effective at supervising the scavenging, never mind persuading frontagers to keep the streets clear of rubbish and other obstructions.

After Man's death, in 1826, Reading had a new Paving Act and a separate Improvement Act and Water Act. Its preamble tells us that under the 1785 Act a lot of money had been spent, debts had mounted, and income was insufficient to pay them off or carry out the necessary works. The new acts authorised increases in rates; provided for further lighting, regulated the laying of gas pipes, and enforced the labelling of streets and the numbering of houses. William Mann (sic) – probably John's son – was one of the new Commissioners.

If John Man were to revisit Reading today he would find a whole new crop of pavement nuisances: parked cars, flying cyclists, wheelie-bins, chewing gum, advertising boards, pub tables, double buggies, charity collectors, market surveyers, opinion pollsters…

The History

Apart from the 1798 map, Man's only publication under his own name was *The History and Antiquities, Ancient and Modern, of the Borough of Reading,* which was largely completed by 1813 but not published until 1816. In his preface he claims that he started work on it before the Rev. Charles Coates's *History* appeared in 1802, but delayed publication so as not to harm Coates's sales. This is plausible, although the historical volume of his *Anecdotes* (see below) was not written up before 1800. Coates had invited subscriptions for his book as early as 1791; in 1792 'the author of the intended history of Reading [presumably Coates] being informed that several collections for the same purpose have been made by gentlemen of the town and neighbourhood, will consider himself as very particularly obliged by any communications which can assist his present undertaking'. It seems that neither Man nor anyone else chose to collaborate; nor did Man subscribe to Coates's book.

Man also claims, fairly, that his work is differently arranged and contains 'new and interesting subjects'. History proper occupies less than a quarter of it, and a third of that is an account of the Civil War. The remaining chapters cover the contemporary town, its churches, trade, militia, charities, MPs, and Corporation – much the same ground as the *Stranger*'s Letter 6 – and there are accounts of current events and doings of no lasting significance. Most commentators have preferred Coates; P H Ditchfield, a later historian, says (in 1888) that Man's *History* is 'poor, unreliable, and full of silly conjectures'.

The Anecdotes

These two bound manuscripts are a very lucky survival, but not an easy read: much of Man's subject-matter is highly topical, his style often convoluted, and his hand neat but tiny. The volume now known as II was kept from 1785 to 1797, and bears an inscription: 'This book is not to be sold – it being a Family Relique. W.M.' Almost the whole content is concerned with satirising local politics, politicians and other public figures. It begins with 'A Paving Song' and a mock-up newspaper called The Paving Miscellany. There is a cod announcement for a play, pieces written in biblical style, and an advert for the sale of 'useless culinary utensils belonging to the Corporation of Gotham'. Later we have 'a series of letters from Dolly the Cook to her Sweetheart in the Country', written, in verse, supposedly in 1644, from Gotham – i.e. Reading. (Gotham is a real village in Nottinghamshire which somehow gained a reputation for the folly of its inhabitants.) 'Editorial' footnotes, as found in the *Stranger,* identify real Reading characters of Man's time. The volume concludes with four items of a different nature, all in verse: a homely piece for New Year's Eve, 1797–98, naming his 'wife so small', his children, and his siblings; 'The Cottage', a tour of Reading's environs which re-appears in the *Stranger's* Letter 7; 'The Counting House' (see 'Barge Man' above), and a poem chastising foolish clergymen.

'Volume I' is inscribed 'by the late J.M.' and headed '*Reading Anecdotes; or, Days of Yore*'. It is a series of essays, numbered (but not in the order of writing) and indexed, and clearly intended for publication; indeed, they are referred to in the *Stranger's* preface and Letter 7. Many are historical, including passages that later appeared in the *History.* There is much gossip; pen-portraits of Reading notables such as Dr Addington and Dr Mitford; and thoughts on Antiquarianism, Metaphors, and Elections. Quite early in the volume he quotes Coates's *History*, which therefore dates most of it post 1802.

A Gentle Man

Many of the *Stranger's* readers over the last two centuries will have perceived its author as a distinctly crabby character, quick to criticise and ready to make enemies, especially in the fields of politics and religion. As to the former, he was complaining about the undemocratic system as much as about its practitioners. In *Parliament through Seven Centuries* (Aspinall et al, 1962) we read that electoral contests at the time were 'little more than struggles for power between individuals belonging to the same class, each backed by a well-stocked purse'. There was 'hardly a hint of division of opinion on the merits of any political question'. In fact Reading's few voters had no real choice in 1806 or 1807, with only two candidates standing for the two seats. The only record of Man's vote we have is for 1820; he supported John Weyland, an anti-party independent. (He was unsuccessful, but was later elected to a rotten borough in Wiltshire; to his credit, he voted for the abolition of his own seat in 1832.) If anything, I would call Man a Radical, for reform and against corruption. He was very likely influenced by William Cobbett, who was intimate with the Mitfords – though I have found no evidence of direct contact between either family and Man. (Cobbett's writings may also have been something of a model for Man's style and his fondness for italics.)

As to religion, Man's harsh words on Methodists and other dissenters do not seem to have been matched by great enthusiasm for the C of E. In a letter of c.1775 he reveals: 'I believe in Christianity because it was founded by a divine power … it has withstood the attacks of deists, and atheists and unbelievers'. My impression is that he held strong and simple views, and worshipped in his own way. The family had its share of tragedy over the years, and his faith certainly helped him at these times of crisis.

Man does not seem to have mingled much with the local Great and Good (or Bad), and we know little of his friendships outside his family and professional associates. But from the limited glimpses afforded by his own unpublished writings, and from the opinions of others, a clear picture emerges:

a kindly, humorous man, a good son, husband and father, popular with his employer, employees and pupils. Above all, he was most certainly his own Man.

BIBLIOGRAPHY

Anon: *Reading Seventy Years Ago* (1887)

Alexander, Alan: *Borough Government and Politics: Reading 1835–1985* (1985)

Childs, W M: *The Town of Reading in the early part of the Nineteenth Century* (1910)

Dearing, John: *The Church That Would Not Die* (1993)

'Detector' (Henry Gauntlett): *Letters to the Stranger in Reading* (1810)

Dibdin, Thomas Frognall: *Reminiscences of a Literary Life* (1836)

Gauntlett, Catherine: *Memoir of the Rev. Henry Gauntlett* (1835)

'Octogenarian' (W S Darter): *Reminiscences of Reading* (1888)

'Philanthropos': *The Compliment Returned to the Stranger in Reading* (1810)

Sawers, Geoff: *Broad Street Chapel* (1996)

Slade, Cecil: *The Town of Reading and its Abbey* (2001)

Histories of Reading by Coates (1802), Doran (1835), Hinton (1954) and Phillips (1999)

Reading Mercury, 1770–1824

Man family website: www.manfamily.org

To the independent, loyal, and enlightened inhabitants of the
Borough of Reading, *this trifle*, is most humbly inscribed
by their obedient servant, and *admirer*, the editor.

Reading, Dec. 29, 1809

PREFACE

The following original Letters having been put into my hands by the gentleman to whom they were addressed, with permission to make what use of them I pleased, I conceived I could not confer a greater favor on my brother townsmen, than by thus submitting them to their perusal.

For tho' the writer has taken great liberties in giving his opinion on some of the subjects here treated on, there is no one but must allow, notwithstanding the boasted superiority of this favorite place, that there are – many parts of it that may be improved – many nuisances that might be removed – and many abuses that call loudly for reformation. Every inhabitant must long have witnessed with regret the shameful state wherein the streets are suffered to remain the year through, either encumbered with the shovellings of the roads, which are seldom taken away, or made the receptacle of all the filth accumulated in the houses. If we look to the pavements, is anything to be seen but – broken stones – overflowing gutters – and the refuse of the pavior left for ever, to encumber the road, and incommode the passenger in his course? These are subjects that seem to have principally engaged the Writer's attention, as no doubt they must every observing Stranger that visits this place; and should the remarks here made be the occasion of the removal of any one of them, the Editor will think himself more than paid for his trouble, even tho' he should thereby have subjected himself to the obloquy of the bigotted and illiberal. His comments on the characters of those writers who have done honor to this their native place, seem to have been dictated by impartiality – his observations on the Corporation, are such as no one can refuse his assent to – and the abuses he has pointed out in the parliamentary representation of the Borough, however unpleasant they may be to the feeling of some, will not, I am convinced, be disapproved of by the great majority of the people. All we have to lament is, that the Writer was not more guarded in his remarks on the character and conduct of the Methodists; but, like all Strangers, who are generally obliged to judge more from what they hear from other persons, than from their own observations, he appears to have imbibed prejudices against these dissenters from the established Church, which have led him to make some observations in regard to them that are not quite correct. Among others, he charges them with being an illiterate *sect, when all the world knows, that those among them who can read, are always poreing over the Scriptures, and* though it may be to no good purpose, *they certainly cannot, with propriety, be called* illiterate, *especially when it is considered, that, in addition to the Bible, many of them peruse that truly pious work the* Evangelical Magazine, *to their very great edification, and* improvement in learning. *To read no books but those on their own side, and to keep no company but those of their own sect, is surely a very* wise *determination, for should they act otherwise, it is much to be feared there would soon be no more Methodists among us; and then, alas! what would become of the world? He also accuses them of* illiberality, *in closing the gates of Heaven to all but themselves; but this is no more than a just policy on their parts, for tho' we are told by an old saying, that the* more the merrier, *yet it also adds, the* fewer the better cheer. *Their want of morality, is another charge he brings against them,* but what, I would ask any reasonable person, have the Saints to do with morality? Is not faith more than sufficient for the fulfilment of all the Christian duties? Did not their great Master die for sinners? and do not they all agree, that the greater the sinner the greater the sacrifice? If this be the case, is it not evident, either that all sinners ought to be Methodists, or that all Methodists must be sinners? These observations I thought necessary to make in behalf of this truly pious sect, against the unjust assertions of the Letter-writer, and trust, that by so doing, I have merited some thanks from a religious society, for which I shall ever retain the greatest respect and admiration.

I am also indebted to the gentleman above mentioned for the Collection of Reading Anecdotes mentioned at the end of the correspondence. These I at first intended to have made part of the present work, but finding they were too voluminous to be comprised in one volume, I have been induced to defer their publication to a future period.

THE EDITOR.

Reading, Oct. 25th, 1809

LETTER 1
arrival from London,
and travel in general

To ⸺⸺⸺⸺⸺

I promised at our parting to give you an account of such occurrences as I might meet with on my travels, as well as such observations as I should from time to time have occasion to make on the present state of society; of men, and manners, and whatever might be most striking in the situation and government of such places as I might be tempted to take up a temporary abode at. In compliance with this engagement I now sit down to give you an account of my arrival at this place, which I reached last night after a pleasant journey of five hours, a rapidity in travelling unknown in former ages, and to which we are in a great measure indebted for the improved state of our turnpike roads, none of which can, I conceive, be in a higher condition than that from the capital to this place. This improvement, you know, took place about the commencement of the last century, before which period the roads in this neighbourhood were nearly impassable for carriages in many places, which seem to have derived their present names from this circumstance, among these may be observed *Slough Lane,* about a mile beyond this town, where I am informed the waggoners coming to market were obliged to wait 'till others came up, to assist them with additional horses, to force their way through the bog: at a little distance

journey of five hours: Stage-coaches hardly improved on this timing in the next 30 years. Fast 'fly-boats' on the Thames were an alternative for those who rated comfort over speed; they cannot have taken much less than two days. A steam-powered road coach made it in three hours in 1835, but it was rail that really shrank the country. Paddington was 65 minutes away in 1840; by 1997 some trains made it in 21 – an average speed of almost 103 mph. It is remarkable that in 2005 there is no bus service from central Reading to London; you have to trek out to a hypermarket 7 kilometres away to catch an occasional coach on its way up from the west.

This improvement: Several Acts of Parliament between 1714 and 1736 enabled the improvement of the Bath Road from Maidenhead to Theale; the Windsor Forest turnpike via Wokingham, Bracknell, Ascot and Virginia Water was set up in 1759.

Slough Lane: This was presumably a local name for a boggy bit of the westbound Bath Road: 'slough' as in despond.

1

farther is a public-house called the *World's End,* to denote, no doubt, that the inhabitants of Reading could seldom extend their excursions beyond this place, which opinion is not quite eradicated at the present day, as many of the tradesmen in their Sunday's walk cannot be *persuaded,* even now, to go beyond it.

There are three ways leading from hence to London, nearly of the same distance, but they are not equally pleasant: that through Windsor Park I should prefer, particularly in the summer season, as the rays of the sun are considerably diminished by the shade of the trees; and the road being generally over the green sward, the passenger is seldom incommoded with dust. But in the winter I always prefer the main Bath road, as from the regular structure of turnpike roads the vehicle is less likely to be jolted from side to side, to the great annoyance of the passengers, as is the case in the summer road: besides the accommodations are better; and the view of the river Thames, in addition to the many country seats, and pleasant villas, with which the road is lined, add considerably to the pleasure of travelling along this busy turnpike road, compared to the dreary scene afforded by thatched hovels and leafless trees in the other. The third road leads through Wokingham, and part of Bagshot Heath to Virginia Water, where it meets the Portsmouth road, but this tract few adopt by choice, either in summer or winter, having nothing to recommend it to the traveller's notice. Wokingham itself, the only town through which it passes, is the most dull, dismal, dreary, place you ever saw, where Poverty seems to have taken up her abode, and from whence the energies of the British character seem to have fled. There are, however, a few good houses in the main street; and the surrounding country, if not remarkably picturesque, is pleasing. Either of these roads you may go or return each day by the established coaches, which are conducted by the proprietors on a very respectable footing: the horses are excellent, and the carriages if not elegant are convenient; they carry six inside passengers, and as many *outside* as the law, or rather the *turnpike keepers,* will allow. This absurd custom of placing the greater part of the weight at the farthest distance from the centre of gravity, whereby many serious accidents have occurred in various parts of the kingdom, has induced a Mr. Milton, a clergyman in this neighbourhood, to invent a coach so constructed as to make it almost impossible for such accidents to happen again, should his plan be generally adopted. The improvement is simply this: A bar extends from the end of each axis between the fore and hind wheels, at the lower extremities of which is a small wheel called an idle wheel, and placed at such a distance from the ground that if either of the main ones should break or come off the idle wheels come into play, and prevent the carriage falling, at the same time that it enables it to continue its progress almost without the passengers being sensible of the change. In addition to this, all the heavy luggage is placed in a receptacle contrived under the body of the coach, which serves as ballast to keep the vehicle in an upright position. A coach was last summer constructed on this principle, and used in turn for a month by each of the proprietors of the coaches here, but from a mistaken notion that it ran heavier than those before in use, neither of them were willing to adopt the plan; in consequence, I have been told, it was disposed of to a coachmaster in the west of England, where it has been constantly used ever since without a single accident having occurred. A proposal has lately

Mr. Milton: Patent no. 2890, filed in 1805 by the Rev. William Milton, vicar of Heckfield, describes his coach. In 1809 the House of Commons appointed a committee to look into road safety; in December 1810 Milton published a Treatise on the Danger of Travelling in Stage-coaches. By October 1811 five of his coaches were running from Reading, and in 1817 we read of 'Mr Milton's Caravan, having all four wheel six feet high, running economically to Marlborough'. Coaches did indeed overturn regularly, and accident reports in the Mercury were often followed by a plug for Milton's invention; but it does not seem to have been widely adopted, perhaps because the Postmater General gave it the thumbs-down.

been made by some of the gentlemen here for entering into a subscription for the encouragement of a *Milton-coach*, to carry four insides with only two outsides, but whether this plan, so much to be desired will take place is as yet uncertain; perhaps the additional expence of fare may prevent its success; if so, I fear the townsmen will long have to regret its failure; for, notwithstanding the care of the present proprietors and drivers of the stage-coaches, and certainly none can exceed them in this respect, serious accidents often do and will occur, from their upsetting, that can only be prevented by having the coaches constructed on this or some similar plan: if therefore the good people of this town should be so careless of their own safety, and so negligent of the lives of their friends and relatives, as to suffer the great benefits to be derived from a coach so constructed to be rejected by them, to whom it was first offered by the inventor, while it is adopted by others, I shall, notwithstanding the high sense I entertain of their understandings, begin to be of the opinion of the traveller, who, after residing here a few days, said, "the farther he travelled westward the more he was convinced the *wise men must have come from the East.*"

I am, &c.
Reading, Sept. 1, 1808

LETTER 2
Reading's first town trail

To ----------------

My curiosity had been so excited by the flattering accounts I had heard of this respectable Borough, that I took the first opportunity that offered of a fine morning, to gratify it, by making an excursion through the principal streets, and I now sit down to give you an account of my observations with that *regard for truth*, you know I am always so anxious to observe, and wherein I shall

"nothing extenuate, nor set down ought in malice!"

The inn from which I now write is situated at the corner of four roads, one of these is that I came in at, but has nothing remarkable in it, except the width of its road way and the paucity of its houses; from this latter circumstance I was at first puzzled to discover why it was dignified with the name of a *street,* 'til I was informed that it was intended to be *one* in another *century or two*, which is you know the *same thing* as if it were *one now*. On the left of this is what may be called a street in the fullest sense of the word, having houses on both its sides, not the most elegant to be sure, but still such as may be deemed comfortable habitations for the poorer classes of the community, who principally reside here. From the *name* of this street it might be supposed to be *paved with silver*, but this *really* is not the case, nor do I believe that an ounce of that

nothing extenuate: these are Othello's words, just before he stabs himself.

The inn: The Crown, a plain brick Georgian building at the top of London Street, was one of the town's two principal coaching inns, and the first to be encountered when arriving from the east. William Pitt stayed there in January 1806, a fortnight before his death. It had its own bowling green, and was the Whig headquarters at election time. In 1825 Joseph Huntley sold biscuits to passengers awaiting fresh horses.

one of these: London Road (New Street on Man's map). The more direct King's Road was not built until 1834.

paucity of its houses: Several pre-Man houses survive, but the big terraces are later.

On the left: Silver Street; Man uses the old form 'Sievier' (sievemaker) on his map.

poorer classes: In 1853 the street was said to house 'prostitutes, thieves, tramps and Irish', and its reputation remained low for decades more.

5

vile flints: Doran's History says that in 1550 the town was paved with flints and round pebbles, 'which rendered the streets, though of themselves broad and stately, very inconvenient to foot passengers'.

metal could be found in the whole street *except* on Saturday night, and even that is sure to take its flight by Monday morning. As to the pavement before the houses I cannot say much in its favor, for though there is on *one side*, for a small distance, a *spacious* piece of flat pavement *almost four inches wide*, the rest is so miserably pitched with vile flints placed with their sharp points upwards, that it is almost impossible for a foot passenger to make his way over them, without either cutting his feet or breaking his legs in the attempt. I was informed on enquiry that this was owing to a *narrowness* of thinking in the Commissioners who superintend this part of the improvements which have of late years been introduced here. The idea adopted by those gentlemen seems to have been, that John Bull has no right to any enjoyments he cannot pay for; and as the inhabitants of this part of the town were incapable of paying the usual rates, they concluded they had no *right* to enjoy the benefits derived from them. But this opinion cannot, I think, be a just one. It is true they have lately been at a great expence in making a *handsome paved foot way* in front of some *large* new built houses, where, from the situation, it could not have been wanted; but this certainly could not have been done merely because the owners *contributed* towards the expence of paving the town, but must have arisen from *some other cause*, though it may not at first sight appear; and therefore I conceive that the miserable state of the pavement above mentioned cannot be owing to a want of means or inclination on the part of the Commissioners to make them better; perhaps they preferred leaving them in their *former state*, to shew to posterity what the whole town was, in this respect, prior to the passing of the paving act.

Having satisfied my curiosity in viewing *every thing* in this part *worth* seeing, which did not *detain* me long, I retraced my steps, and turning again to the left, passed the inn I had just left, part of which projects considerably into the high road, and, thus reducing it in breadth, prevents the possibility of making a footpath for the conveniency and safety of the passengers, who are in consequence obliged to keep the high road, unless they *prefer* being *crushed to death* against a long brick wall (which is continued from the inn the whole length of the street) by some of the numerous carriages that are every minute passing and repassing this way, it being the greatest thoroughfare in the town. A few winters back, one of the night coaches, endeavouring to turn the corner in this narrow passage, was literally dashed to pieces against a post; several of the passengers were hurt, and the coachman had his leg broken. This accident roused the attention of the Commissioners of the Road, and they immediately offered the proprietor of the inn a very large sum of money, to be permitted to take down the projecting part of the inn and the brick wall, so as to enable them, from a part of the garden, to widen the road, and render it safe and commodious for every description of travellers. I have not heard why this scheme was not carried into effect, but from whatever quarter the opposition to so necessary a measure arose, were I the party who caused it, I should consider every future accident that may happen from its rejection, as imputable to my want of *philanthropy*, or to some worse motive.

After passing through this dangerous passage, I came to two cross ways, that to the left leads out of the town, and has towards its summit a few respectable houses, very *conveniently*

high road: Crown Street, also New Street on the map. Many coaches came along here and down Southampton Street to avoid congestion on the High Bridge.

that to the left: Southampton Street

brick kiln: Waugh's kiln was established at Katesgrove by 1802, and Sherman's was somewhere near the present Sherman Road.

de gustibus: 'There's no disputing about tastes.'

situated to receive the *volumes of smoke* constantly issuing from a neighbouring brick kiln, whose effluvia, however *gratifying* it may be to the natives of this place, would to me, who am a stranger, be considered the greatest of nuisances; but *de gustibus*, you know, *non est disputandum.*

On the right, is a wide street, with some handsome new built houses; these being set back from the original line of buildings on that side the way, and having small courts or gardens in the front of each, enclosed with a palisado, give a lightness and airiness to this street which is not observable in any other part of the town. On the opposite side the way, which is more convenient for foot passengers, the houses are not so good, but the pavement is uncommonly wide, increasing as you advance, 'till it is obstructed by the church-yard jutting considerably into the road, and forming a nook or corner, which a neighbouring brick-layer, *very properly*, no doubt, has either been permitted, or *has assumed*, the right of converting into a receptacle for his building materials, so that the passenger may, at his *option*, either *break his neck* over a pile of loose flints, or souse *over head and ears* in a heap of new made mortar. As I did not choose to do either, I took a stroll into the church-yard, in hopes of finding some memorial worth recording, such as that of

Removed from over the way,

which I am told was not long since inscribed on one of the tomb-stones, but is now taken away, as savouring, perhaps, of too much levity on so serious a subject.

Being disappointed in my expectations here, I continued my route by the church-yard wall, at the end of which a baker had *very obligingly* placed two large barrows, for the accommodation of those who might wish to be *under the surgeon's hands*; but those who might not be desirous of so *great a blessing*, I found, might easily pass along, by only *stepping up to their knees in the puddle of water* running down the gutter

On the right: Southampton Street (Horn Street on the map)

handsome new built houses: The present nos. 78–84, formerly known as Southampton Place, with their pioneering front gardens, built by the Richard Billings, father and son.

pavement is uncommonly wide: The pavement still widens on the east side.

church-yard: St Giles

Removed from over the way: this cannot be a reference to the overflow graveyard across the street, which was not inaugurated until 1819.

the usual tract: Bridge Street. The IDR and the Oracle make it hard to imagine this area in Man's day; but none of the early maps suggest that there was much danger of walking into St Giles's millstream. He would no doubt have something to say about the circuitous route that pedestrians are now obliged to take here, and might take comfort from the proposed demolition of the flyover.

large inn: the Bear, the other principal coaching inn. Coleridge had stayed there in 1794 when he was trying to join the army to pay off his debts, using the alias Silas Tomkyn Cumberbache; in Man's day it was a haunt of Tories. Man does not mention Simonds' brewery, a large building of 1790 by Soane, which would have dominated this area.

wide handsome street: Castle Street.

The curve line: The gentle S-curve is preserved in Reading's finest streetscape on the south side; the raw, blocky straightness of the 1977 Magistrates' Courts and Police Station opposite ruins the effect. The view up into Castle Hill is now interrupted by the well-intentioned trees on the IDR roundabout.

gentlemen, or tradesmen: Man himself lived here.

that separates the path from the high road; and then resume the usual tract, which, if they happen to *be blind*, will lead them *directly into the mill stream*; but those who can *see*, generally *prefer* turning a little to the left, which leads them over several small bridges, where the road becomes narrower, but this inconvenience is *compensated* by the additional quantity of mud that is continually accumulating, owing to the air and the rays of the sun being excluded by some lofty poplars on one side, and the elevated walls of a large inn on the other; nevertheless such is the *perversity* of mankind, that the landlord has actually taken *a dislike* to this accumulation of filth before his house, and is in the habit of sending his servants to remove it to the opposite side, where finding its level in the path, it forms a *very soft* and *refreshing* walk for the foot-passengers, who, for this reason, I suppose, generally *prefer* this side of the way.

Taking the next turning to the left, I proceeded along a wide handsome street, leading, as I was told, to Bath. The curve line, which, you know, is esteemed the line of beauty, is adopted here in most if not all the streets, but particularly in this, which is in the form of an *S*. Most of the houses being inhabited by gentlemen, or tradesmen out of business, the shops are few in number, and in consequence the street is less encumbered with obstructions; but I could not help remarking a custom, which, however *odd* it may appear to strangers, is almost universally adopted here: I mean, that of having a *pretty little* dunghill before each house, composed of road dirt, ashes, straw, dung, turnip parings, cabbage leaves, &c. &c. but these last are not so plentiful as might be *wished*, owing to some all-devouring hogs, who are continually plundering these precious compounds of the greater part of *their beauty*. It is true that by express orders of the Paving Committee, hogs are forbid *taking an airing* in the streets, but this, like many other salutary measures, is wholly neglected, and the consequence is, the streets are not only *much cleaner* than they *ought* to be, in the opinion of the people, if we may judge from the pains they take to make them otherwise; but every housekeeper is thereby deprived of the pleasure of imbibing the effluvia of rotten vegetables. At the extremity of this street are two very neat toll-houses, where the line of buildings ends; few people, for obvious reasons, being willing to build beyond them. I therefore took down a narrow lane, and through a very neat nursery garden, which brought me to another outlet of the town leading to Oxford. In this quarter,

toll-houses: The stretch of the Bath Road westwards from this point was Reading's first turnpike, set up in 1714. The toll system petered out by the 1860s; now we charge vehicles to enter cities, not to leave them.

a narrow lane: Back Lane, which was obliterated when Russell and Baker Streets were built from the 1820s. Pig's Green Lane on the map was usually known as Peg's, and became the Tilehurst Road.

another outlet: the Oxford Road (Pangbourne Road on the map).

the houses are extending: Speculative building was just beginning to spread in this direction; the more prestigious developments along the King's and London Roads and Eldon Square came later.

the act for regulating buildings: London builders had been subject to Acts and regulations since 1189; most were concerned with preventing the spread of fire, but from 1667 they introduced quality controls and standard designs for four classes of house. Provincial builders usually followed suit.

Entering the town: Man passed along what became Oxford Street, then part of the Oxford Road, and eventually (for commercial reasons) Broad Street West.

I turned to the left: West Street.

another of greater extent: Friar Street.

the town bridewell: Greyfriars church, which lacks the usual Reading chequered flint and stonework but has certainly had a chequered history. Built in 1311, it later served as a Town Hall and then a Bridewell until 1844. It was rebuilt and reconsecrated in 1863, and its elegant nave arcade is one of the most beautiful things in town.

the houses are extending very fast, but I was sorry to observe such a mixture of apparently good and inferior buildings, all jumbled together without order or regularity; and what was worse, to find them composed of much too slight materials to be durable. It is a pity that the act for regulating buildings within the bills of mortality is not in force at this place.

Entering the town by this road, I turned to the left through a wide but short street, which led to another of greater extent; at the west end of it, is the town bridewell, originally a conventual church of the grey friars, given to the Corporation by Henry VIII. at the dissolution, for the purpose of making it a Town-hall, but afterwards they having obtained a more eligible situation for their Hall, this was converted to its present use.

The prison is about 80 feet long by 54 wide, consisting of the original body and side aisles of the church, the chancel having been taken down some years. The former is divided into 2 wards by a boarded transept, separating the male from the female prisoners, and open at the top, the roof of the church having been recently taken down to prevent its falling. The south aisle was, 'till lately, the keeper's house, and the north one has been converted into cells for the prisoners, opening into the body of the church, where they are allowed to walk. On the same side are 3 solitary cells, lately erected beyond the original line of the building, on the north side, but communicating with the prison by doorways formed in the original wall. These cells are about 14 feet long by 6 wide, to which is added a small court yard, about 7 feet square. The cells, it is true, are lined with wood, but neither light nor air are admitted into them when the door is closed on their wretched *inhabitants*, and the only furniture they possess is *a bed of straw*. The courtyards are paved with bricks, which are always green and damp, from the exclusion of the sun and air by the surrounding walls. Such are the places which the Corporation has provided for those unhappy beings, who, from want, or the infirmity of our natures, have been impelled to transgress the laws. The ingenuity of mankind, one would have supposed, could not have contrived a place so well adapted to reduce their fellow men below the condition of their beasts, who, tho' compelled to labor, are *oftentimes* better fed and *more comfortably* lodged. In these holes the wretched sufferer is compelled to linger for 3, 6, and sometimes twelve months on the scanty prison allowance of bread and water, without a bed to lie on, and even deprived of fire in the coldest months of winter, at the same time that they are exposed to the inclemency of the season, in a place never dry, and from whence, at their release, they will probably carry with them the seeds of disorders that may render their future days full of pain and misery. With a wish that some future Howard, guided by humanity, might be tempted to visit this dismal abode of misery, and by the influence of his character, might prevail with the magistrates, at least, to ameliorate, if not entirely remove it, I hastened away, and pursued my walk along the main street, without meeting any thing worth noticing, except *filling my shoes* at every step from the *puddle water* that lay concealed under the *beaux-traps*; this you may suppose was very *cooling* and *refreshing* at this season of the year. These traps are so *numerous*, and so ingeniously contrived by the pavior, that those who walk the streets, in whatever part of the town it may be, may at all times be accommodated with a *cold bath* on the *shortest notice*. At the end of the street is

some future Howard: John Howard (1726–90), prison reformer, was instrumental in getting the 1774 Gaol Act through Parliament, though it was not always enforced. He did visit the old Castle Street gaol in 1779.

any thing worth noticing: The few pre-Man buildings that survive are all small houses with modern shopfronts. Most are Listed, an accolade denied to more distinctive edifices such as the late Boar's Head and ABC cinema, and the surviving display of terracotta on the former Athanaeum Club.

beaux-traps: a nonce-word that didn't make it into the *OED*; presumably he means loose paving-stones.

Town-hall: Designed by Charles Poulton, Alderman and cabinet-maker, in 1785; now perversely called the Victoria Hall, hidden behind Waterhouse's 1875 frontage. The plain eighteenth-century east flank was visible from St Laurence's churchyard until Messrs Blandy & Blandy extended their bland offices.

the Town-hall, a neat unornamented building, in the shape of a parallelogram. At each end are the courts of justice, so contrived, that while from the usual echo of a large room, you are prevented from hearing the evidence in that, wherein you are sitting, you may, without moving from your situation, *derive amusement* from the *pleadings of the counsel* in the other. Here is held the Mayor's annual feasts, and other public dinners, for which purpose ample offices are provided under the building. But you are not to suppose from this, that the people here are *gormandizers*, so far from it, it is well known how *patiently* they submitted to go without their annual feasts year after year while the Corporation *was out at elbows*: and even *now*, judging from the *small number* that sit down to dinner at this great civic feast, it is supposed that not *one half of those invited attend*, otherwise they would, as on *former occasions*, be more numerous. Here also are held the assemblies and coteries, which in the winter season are numerously attended, as well by the higher classes resident in the town, as by the nobility and gentry of the environs. Adjoining the Town-hall is the council-chamber, where the magistrates of the town hold a court of record every Wednesday, for the adjustment of trifling disputes and other business. In this room are many pictures of persons who have been benefactors to the town, but most of them in a wretched style, particularly that of Queen Elizabeth.

Leaving the Town-hall, I passed by a very venerable looking Church, which I was sorry to see had lately been disfigured by some paltry gingerbread ornaments of angels, and I know not what, stuck on each side the grand entrance door way, wholly incongruous with the simplicity of the original building. Thus you find even this place has its Goths and Vandals, who, prompted by a barbarous taste, in endeavouring to improve, destroy, the purity and simplicity of the architecture adopted with so much chastness and propriety by our ancestors. But this is not the only deformity this church has been destined to undergo, for on the south side, which fronts the Market-place, a most clumsy and ill-formed arcade or corridor has been erected, in defiance of every rule of architecture; a receptacle for idleness and vice, and where, I am told, midnight orgies are held, unbecoming the sacredness of the place, and impeaching the vigilance of the magistrates.

At the east end of this strange building, but in a line with it, in front, is a small prison very characteristically called the *hole*, where disturbers of the peace, and disorderly persons are confined previous to their being examined by the magistrates

a very venerable looking Church: St Laurence. What would Man think of the 2004 internal re-ordering, with its steel-and-glass coffee-bar intended to attract Youth?

paltry gingerbread ornaments: The niches beside the west door formerly held statues of Saints Laurence and Vincent; they were removed before 1802, and in 1806 the whole tower was coated with Roman cement (which had been invented in 1796) and some of the old carvings were reproduced in this material.

a most clumsy and ill-formed arcade: The Piazza, paid for posthumously by John Blagrave in 1619. Originally known as The Walke, it later borrowed the Italian name from Inigo Jones's pioneering square (1630) at Covent Garden; the word was here illiterately applied to an arcade which did not enclose or face an open space. It obscured the south aisle windows, and was demolished in 1868. George Hillier, in his own 'Stranger' book, called this an act of vandalism.

at the Compter, on the opposite side the way. These two prisons were, 'till lately, united by a gateway leading into the Forbury, over which was a place of confinement for debtors, but the Corporation having been deprived, by a late act of parliament, of the power granted them by their Charter, of enforcing the payment of small debts, the prison has been removed, and the opening into the Forbury rendered more commodious. Next to this is a small aisle, communicating withinside with the church, formerly the pew and burial place of the ancient family of the Knollys, many of whom, at different times, represented this borough in Parliament, down to 1760, when it became extinct in Sir Francis Knollys, bart. the last Member of that family. Were all these buildings to be taken down, which might be done at a small expence, and without detriment to any one, the south side of the church might be so improved by additional doors and windows, and other ornaments, in consonance with the rest of the building, as to form a pleasing object on entering the Market-place from any part of the town, as well as improve the entrance, which is now too narrow, into one of the pleasantest spots in the county. This is called the Forbury: on the south and west sides it is enclosed with houses, a part of the church-yard, and the magnificent ruins of the Abbey, which have hitherto bade defiance to devouring time, and the still more destructive energies of man. On the north is a long terrace walk, bounded by a low wall, affording a delightful view of the Oxfordshire hills, clothed with woods, interspersed with rich corn fields, and gentlemen's seats, extending one beyond the other as far as the eye can reach. Between the hills and the town is a fine fertile valley, through which Old Father Thames majestically

the Forbury: The best house was no. 22, built c.1690 and disgracefully knocked down in 1962 to make room for a smelly urban motorway inside a terrible office block. The road never happened, and the block has itself given way to Forbury Square.

a long terrace walk: Now you can see little more than offices, trees and the railway embankment.

16

but slowly winds along, seeming to cast a longing lingering eye on this place, from which, though within so short a distance, he has for ages been excluded. Following the river eastward, with the eye, we see it gradually disappear behind the hills, and again, while passing round a promontory, emerging into sight, thus alternately appearing and disappearing, 'till it is finally concealed from the enraptured spectator, by the rich foliage of the surrounding country. Charming as this spot is, its beauties are all lost to the inhabitants; you will hardly credit the assertion, when I tell you, this delightful terrace is for a great way bordered by an enormous dunghill, formed by the scavenger and the nightman. The road leading through it is mended, or rather deteriorated, with broken bricks, tiles, &c. &c. collected from the ruins of old buildings, laid up in this place, by different workmen, who seem to consider it rather as a deposit for their rubbish than a promenade, as it ought to be, for the ladies. In front of the houses is a plot of grass of a semicircular form, in part surrounded with palisadoes, and in part by a muddy ditch, the general receptacle of dead dogs, cats, and carrion of all kinds, sufficient to breed a pestilence in this otherwise salubrious spot. Attempts have at times been made to improve this pleasant place but without effect, as must be the case, 'till the Corporation remove the fairs, annually held here, to a more convenient situation, and where the youths also of the town may be indulged without molestation, to enjoy their pastimes as they have been allowed to do here for two centuries past. At the eastern extremity of the Forbury is the County Gaol and Bridewell, a modern brick building, on Mr. Howard's plan. In the front is the keeper's house, and at a small distance behind it, is a very neat

Attempts have at times been made: Cecil Slade's book on relations between Town and Abbey charts the history of this site from the 1539 Dissolution to the 2004 lottery-funded restoration. By 1810 the ruins were no longer being deliberately destroyed; antiquaries were poking about, but there was little attempt to actively preserve what was left. The Forbury, used for fairs and military parades, was undoubtedly a mess; though in 1774 a Town Hall Ball raised funds to improve it, and the Hill was fenced in 1799 to make a pleasure-ground. Joshua Vines had another go at beautifying it in 1831 – as recorded on a plaque – and the Council finally acquired the whole site in 1854 after campaigning by (among others) the great George Lovejoy.

County Gaol: The one Man saw dated from 1793, but lasted only 50 years; although it boasted such luxuries as in-cell privies, it was badly built and soon overcrowded. Moffat and Scott's classic cruciform design replaced it in 1843. You have to be a Young Offender to get inside now, but a good idea of its galleried layout can be obtained in the main mall of the Oracle shopping centre.

chapel, where the church service is performed every Sunday. The rest of the building, in the form of a square, contains the different wards and cells, which are furnished with every necessary convenience that can be expected in such places; so that even solitary confinement here is rendered much less irksome than in the Town Bridewell, and the cells being perfectly dry, from their exposure to the sun and air, the health of the convict is not undermined, tho' his spirits, as was intended, may be broken. Behind the wards is a large court yard, surrounded by a high wall, but open to the sun; here the prisoners occasionally walk, or when sentenced to hard labor, are employed in sawing stone, wood, or such other work as can be procured for them. Round the outer wall of the prison is a garden, enclosed with another wall, but lower, where some of the convicts are occasionally employed: at such times, and I believe from their first entering the prison, they are dressed in party colored clothes, half blue, half yellow, from head to foot, except the shoes. This method has been adopted, as well to render their escape more difficult, as to prevent infectious diseases being introduced into the Gaol, by means of their own dresses; these, in the mean time, are carefully fumigated with brimstone, in an iron stove provided for that purpose, and returned to them when going to be tried or discharged. On leaving the prison, I returned the way I came into the Market-place; this is nearly of a triangular form, and kept very neat and clean, at the expence of the Corporation, who thus set an example which the different parishes in the town would do well to follow. On each side are shops decorated in the best style, where goods of every description may be had as cheap as in London. Nearly in the

Market-place: Some pre-Man buildings survive; the dreadful 1960s scheme on concrete pillars was halted in its tracks by Reading Civic Society.

centre is a large stone *lamp post*, if such it may be called, of a triangular form, to correspond, I suppose, with that of the Market-place, but of what order of architecture, I was not able to discover; some of the ornaments however are British, some Roman, and some Egyptian. The base, or pedestal, is, as you may conclude from its shape, divided into three compartments, in one of which, composed of the same kind of ginger-bread work I mentioned before, are the town arms, consisting of five maidens' heads placed lozenge wise, the middle one crowned, the others ornamented with garlands of flowers; but I was informed by a *great antiquary*, who resides here, that this was not correct, the original arms having been five maidens' heads, *veiled as nuns*, and not in the meretricious dresses they are here represented; as to the middle one being crowned, he says, it was only introduced in compliment to Queen Elizabeth, who was a great benefactress to the town, and consequently might very well now be omitted. In another compartment are the arms of the founder, and in the third an inscription on a brass plate, recording the time of its erection.

a large stone *lamp post*: The Simeon obelisk (1804) is now more commonly called the Soane monument, the designer having achieved more lasting fame than the donor. Simeon's first idea was for a square, four-lamp design. It was the subject of satirical verses in the *Mercury* in 1806, some of which may have been written by Man. After many years of neglect it is finally being restored, and the ugly public loos removed.

town arms: The Arms, with a queen among four maids, were granted in 1566; before that Reading had only a Common Seal, showing a king with a Saxon crown (possibly Edward of England, 975–78) and four men.

The three facets, or corners of the base, are ornamented with what I at first mistook for *bundles of sticks* or *fagots*, with a woodman's axe thrust into the ends of each of them; but the same learned gentleman assured me, that they were intended to represent the fasces and axes usually carried before the Roman Consuls, in token of their *supreme* power; if so, they are certainly not appropriately introduced here, as the Corporation have only a *delegated*, not a supreme power; they may *whip*, but not *behead* an offender: I would therefore recommend that the axes be taken away, and the fasces left, as being all that is classically necessary to represent that degree of power the Corporation really possess. On the pedestal is raised a triangular shaft, with the facets ornamented in the Egyptian style, and surmounted at the top with something *like an acorn*. At each corner of the pedestal is a large lamp, for the maintenance whereof, for ever, I am told, the founder has funded a sufficient sum of money in annuities, under the management of the Corporation. It is surrounded by a handsome iron railing, and may, upon the whole, be called a pretty, rather than a correct, design for a lamp post.

Leaving the Market-place, I turned up a narrow street, on my right hand, formed by one broad street being divided into two, by a row of houses built longitudinally, nearly half its length. There was a proposal made, some years ago, by some of the inhabitants of the town, to purchase and take down the whole row, which might then have been done at a small expence, several of the houses being in a dilapidated state, but the scheme getting vent, most of the tenants purchased their own houses, and rebuilt many of them, thus putting it out of the power of the *schemers* to remove them, as proposed; how-

like an acorn: this is in fact a pine-cone, which Soane intended to be made of bronzed or gilded copper.

At each corner: Simeon intended the lamps to be lit in perpetuity. Oil gave way to gas in 1883; darkness reigned from 1911 to 1971, when electrified mock gas lamps appeared, soon replaced by hanging baskets. There is now to be light again.

one broad street: The north side of Broad Street was Butcher Row, the south Fish Row.

ever, they still flatter themselves, that this improvement may take place prior to the *millennium*, if not within a century or two. Near the entrance of this street is a handsome new-built Market-house, for butchers' meat, poultry, butter, eggs, &c. It is a long square, communicating with the Market-place at the north-eastern extremity, and divided into two compartments by a row of butchers' shops running along the middle, from one extremity to the other; fronting which is another row, with a passage between them. In the other division is the fowl-market; both are very well supplied on the Saturday, which is the general market day here, though there is another on Wednesdays. Possessed of so convenient a market-house in nearly the heart of the town, it is astonishing that the green-grocers, and others, should be permitted, in the manner they do, to obstruct the highways with their stalls, which are to be seen in every street, with baskets of potatoes, and other vegetables, placed on the foot-ways, for those who *choose* to tumble over them, in addition to the nuisance arising from their refuse, being left to rot in the streets. This, and the opposite, street is so narrow, that two carriages cannot pass at a time in either of them; on which account the footways are obliged to be proportionally narrow, notwithstanding this, many of the shopkeepers have been allowed to throw out bow-windows to their shops; these, overhanging the path, oblige the foot-passengers to walk the greater part of the way in the high road, among carts and carriages, but if this is attended with *difficulty* and *danger*, he is amply *compensated* by the *great pleasure* he must feel on viewing, as he goes along, the different *slaughter-houses* on either side the way. Here, he may see the patient ox, after a life of labor and toil, for the benefit of the

this improvement: the clearance was eventually made in 1862.

Market-house: There is a description of the 'lately built' Market-house in Man's History. Hillier described it as inadequate in 1859.

bow-windows: the word first appeared in 1753, though bays and oriels were common long before that. Under the 1774 Building Act they were not to project more than ten inches.

Readingensian: John Blagrave called himself 'Readingensum'; Man's may be the first use of the anglicized form of the word.

turning on the left: St Mary's Butts. Until the 1880s the church was hemmed in by almshouses on this side.

I soon came to a church: St Mary's, now known as the Minster.

a few monuments: notably William Kendrick (1635) who built some almshouses in Silver Street.

graves are not kept: They continue to crumble, though some are Listed Structures.

human race, ignominiously and brutally dragged by the horns to the slaughter: there, another just expiring, from a blow directed by an unerring arm, and from the blood which flows like a torrent from his severed wind-pipe, while the air resounds with his groans. In another part he may behold the unfeeling butcher *twisting the tail* and *screwing down the head* of the innocent calf, still moaning after its dam, while the fatal knife is piercing his throat: or the harmless sheep, and bleating lamb, almost flayed alive, and their entrails torn out, as a reward for having clothed their ungrateful masters from their own backs. Add to this, rivers of blood flowing in the kennels, and then say, if any *inconvenience* can be too great to undergo for such a *gratification?* I mean as to a Readingensian, whose sensibilities do not appear to me to be of the finer sort, otherwise I should think a sight like this would not be suffered in the heart of so great a town; as for myself, I must confess my feelings are not yet sufficiently callous to allow me to partake of such scenes with pleasure: I therefore made the best of my way to the end of the broader part of the street; when, turning on the left, I soon came to a church, of a fanciful, though not unpleasing, structure; the tower, which is square, being composed of alternate compartments of flints and free-stone, each about a foot square, something like a tessellated pavement. The body of the church has nothing remarkable in it, except a few monuments, among which are two or three to former benefactors of the town. The church-yard is extensive, and *well* filled, but I am sorry to say, the graves are not kept in such order as decency requires. One thing I could not help noticing, that whereas in all other places the dead are buried, lying *East* and *West*, here they are placed in almost all directions, except full North and South, as if, like *vessels at sea*, they could, at all times, make their *destined port*, with *a side wind*. On enquiry, however, I found, that those who are placed out of the common direction were methodists, which accounts for this singularity. On the south side the Church-yard, they have began taking down some old houses to widen the road; and I am assured, from good authority, that the remainder will actually follow in something *more than half a century*; so that you see the good people of this county metropolis cannot, with propriety, be charged with making, as some people do, *more haste than speed*; as what in other places would be accomplished in twelve months, will take here more than *one century to talk about it, another to put it in train*, and a *third to finish it*. My attention was attracted at this place by observing some labourers busily employed in demolishing an altar tomb, that appeared venerable from its antiquity. I was informed it had, for nearly four centuries, protected the remains of one John Leche, *alias* John of the Larder; by which appellation he is generally known; though it was only a *soubriquet* given him, in his life time, from his office of purveyor of the Abbey. It appeared that some of those people properly called Goths, who abound in all places, conceiving the tomb in question to be in the way of some improvements they were making, had ordered it to be taken down, on their own assumed authority. When this shameful violation was complained of by some of the more enlightened inhabitants, their reply was, if you can *prove* it to have been John-â-Larder's tomb, we will cause it to be rebuilt: thus pretending to doubt of a fact, which they, as well as every other man in the town, knew to be true, from unerring

placed in almost all directions: almost all of the graves do, in fact, lie pretty well east-west. But some of the older ones may have been replaced by new burials after 1810.

methodists: I have not found any evidence for this claim. Burial-space was at a premium until the Cemetery opened in 1843; two-fifths of it was allocated to Reading's many Dissenters.

what in other places: This quip, which probably crops up in other towns, was quoted (without acknowledgement) by John Okey Taylor, mayor-elect, in 1862.

John of the Larder: John Leche, known as John a Larder, was some sort of quartermaster at the Abbey. In 1475 he founded some almshouses in the Butts.

a *Kenrick*, an *Aldworth*, or a *West*: John Kendrick (brother of William), who died in 1624, left money to found the Oracle workhouse (which Man walks past, without comment, a few minutes later); Richard Aldworth left £4000 in 1646 to set up the Blue Coat School, which was further endowed by John West (d 1723).

tradition, handed down from father to son, to the present day; besides this testimony, they knew, that the Corporation, if they did not originally cause it to be erected, have, ever since, made it the duty of their Chamberlains to keep it in repair, in memory of the man, who laid the foundation-stone of those numerous charities, for the benefit of the poor of all descriptions, which abound in this town. It was, perhaps, from this tomb, that the first idea arose in the minds of a *Kenrick*, an *Aldworth*, or a *West*, of devoting the greater part of their fortunes to charitable purposes, like this their prototype, around whose tomb they had sported in their youth, and whose pious intentions they recollected, and emulated in old age.------ From its height from the ground, this monument had long served, if it had not originally been so intended, for a resting place for porters, and others, to deposit their burthens; but, even this charitable purpose, so grateful to hearts capable of feeling for their fellow men, whose situations in life oblige them to become, as it were, beast of burthen for others, who have been more fortunate, could not shelter it from the destructive hand of daring delapidators. So long as this monument remained, to commemorate the founder; so long have the neighbouring alms-houses, with the several estates, given by the founder, for the maintenance of their poor inmates, been kept sight of by the inhabitants of the town: it is now removed from their observation, and we know not how soon the name of the man may be forgotten, and his foundation, like that of his grave, be violated, by sacrilegious hands. You will ask me, perhaps, what the Corporation, who, in a great measure, owe their present consequence to the example set by John-â-Larder, have done, to vindicate his ashes? or to punish this wanton violation of the rights of the dead? *Nothing*! What the Church, with her white sheets, her decretals, her bulls, and her anathemas? *Nothing*! No one has come forward to call the act in question. The gratitude of the Corporation is sunk in apathy! the People want spirit to resent it! and the Church seems very willing to overlook this profanation of the ashes of departed worth, committed to her protection, in ground *hallowed* for the purpose, and, as at the present day, purchased for a considerable price, by John-â-Larder's executors!

Crossing the Church-yard, I entered another narrow street, in a part where half a dozen fat hogs were hanging across the foot-path, apparently just killed, with their reeking entrails hanging on each side; fortunately, as the path here was tolerably wide, I got by, without stumbling into the yawning

another narrow street: Various schemes for widening Gun Street were put forward from 1803 onwards, but not much happened until the houses on the churchyard side were demolished in 1816.

bellies of either of them; which seemed capable of receiving *one* much larger than myself. After a few more incumbrances, I came to another pork-shop, in the narrowest part of the street; but here I was not so fortunate, for, in endeavouring to pass between the shop and a carriage, I brought away with me nearly *half a pint of blood* in my coat sleeve, and very prettily laced my new beaver with hogs' lard; a convincing proof that in this famous place, "*everyone doeth that which is good in his own eyes*," if he considers it to be for his own advantage; without paying any attention to decency, good order, or the convenience and comfort of his neighbours. Passing on, my attention was drawn to a bookseller's shop window, but while I was perusing the titles of the books exposed for sale, I inadvertently overset a whole row of *earthen-ware*, that, notwithstanding the narrowness of the foot-path, had been ranged along the ground in the front of the next house. Disgusted with repeated disasters, I made the best of my way out of the street, but not without apprehension of some of the houses falling on my head; they having been apparently built in the *glorious days of good Queen Bess*, with one story over-hanging the other, in the usual manner of those times, 'till they nearly met at the roof. These, also, I am informed, are intended to be purchased by the town, and the entrance of the street widened, but as no *period* is fixed for its being done, I suppose it will be *ad Calendas Græcas*. I should have mentioned a large two-wheeled barrow, belonging to the grocer at the corner, but as this is generally placed in the high road, for the apparent purpose of *overturning carts and carriages*, and not with the *kind* intention of furnishing the foot-passengers with *broken legs*, it appeared to be out of my line of observation.

a bookseller's shop window: Robert Snare had opened his Minster Street shop in 1790.

good Queen Bess: there is little of her time to be seen in town now, and none here.

ad Calendas Graecas: i.e. never – the Greeks had no calends in their calendar.

26

On the right, is a wide street, communicating at each end
with the Market-place; here are some very good shops; but
the turning, at the bottom, into the next street, is so narrow,
as hardly to admit of one carriage at a time, and even that must
keep a line of draft in the form of an *S* to enter it; I have not

On the right: King Street.

been able to learn when this entrance is to be widened; but I have heard it *whispered* about, that one member of the C——— has been actually *looking* at it, and that *another* has been heard to say, he would subscribe *five farthings* towards it. The street itself, though one of the greatest thoroughfares in the town, is very narrow, and consequently liable to constant stoppages, by carts and carriages loading and unloading, at the several shops on each side of it. At the end of this street is a neat stone bridge, of one arch, lately erected by the Corporation, but so unfortunately placed, that the trading barges, which are very long here, are obliged to pass under it in a diagonal direction, owing to an island situated within a few yards above, and opposite the arch way. A proposal was made, a few years since, to obtain an act of parliament for the purpose of improving the navigation of the Kennet, in this part, and in its further passage through the town, the very worst, perhaps, that this country can produce, being not only exceedingly crooked and narrow, but also so shallow, as to render it impossible to navigate boats, fully laden, along its present channel; and, to add to these inconveniences, towing the boats by horses, a method adopted in every other part of the navigation, is obliged to be dropt here, because the adjoining lands are all private property. This proposition, so desirable for the improvement of the town, as well as for the advantages expected from it to the navigator, was prevented, by the interference of the proprietor of the river, but, on what grounds, I am yet to learn.

From the bridge, you enter a street of considerable width, with very few shops in it, so that the traveller meets with fewer impediments to his progress here, than in the other parts of the town; however, I could not help noticing the *modesty* of

a neat stone bridge: High Bridge, built by Robert Brettingham of London in 1787.

a diagonal direction: The Kennet had been navigable to Newbury since 1723. An extension to Bath was mooted in 1770, but not until 1788 was a committee formed to set up the Kennet and Avon canal company; had the scheme been further advanced by 1787, the High Bridge might have taken a more convenient form. Navigating the length upstream from here (the Brewery Gut) without a towpath was slow and difficult. To get a boat up through the bridge, some sort of tackle was attached, with the horse walking downstream; a long rope was then floated down from Bridge Street. The Oracle has opened it out, but the section is still controlled by traffic lights, and stopping is, alas, not allowed. As we have seen, Man had a professional interest in waterborne transport; it is odd that he does not mention the imminent opening of the whole canal.

a street of considerable width: London Street, which would then have looked as splendid as Ludlow's Broad Street still does. It still has few shops proper, though the Georgian, Victorian and neo-Georgian houses are mostly in commercial use; there is too much traffic, and quantities of signboards spoil the effect.

one shop-keeper, who had taken the liberty of placing on the pavement, in front of his house, about two dozen butter firkins, oozing out at every joint of the staves; opposite these, so as to leave a space of about a foot wide for passengers, were several hundred weight of cheese, placed likewise in a row; a barrel of herrings, chests of tea, empty sugar hogsheads, a barrel of tar, half a dozen sides of bacon, two dozen hams, a tub of red herrings, one of corks, two large wheel-barrows, and a pair of shop-steps; by these means rendering it as impossible for any one to *forget the situation* of his shop, as for the most cautious passenger to pass through this chaos without bringing away some *token* of the different articles the gentleman deals in. On the same side the way, I met with an obstruction of a different kind: on my right hand was ranged a quantity of second-hand houshold furniture, and on my left was *a cellar window*, wide open, and extending nearly across the footpath; to pass these, without danger, was impossible; I therefore crossed over to my inn, took a hearty, and well-dressed, dinner, and then sat down to give you the above account of my peregrinations; which, I fear, you are by this time heartily tired of. I therefore conclude, with my best wishes.

Your's, &c.
Reading, ------------

LETTER 3
on paving, water, umbrellas, hawkers, insurance,
drama, beer, medicines, dialect, baldness,
attornies and begging

To ----------------

I hinted in my last, at the broken and imperfect state of the pavement in this town; whether the Commissioners are sleeping, or only want jogging, I know not; but it seems to be high time they were roused, lest they fall into the *pits* they have left for others, or break their necks by tripping against the fragments of broken stones, in many places overtopping the level of the adjoining pavement several inches, in which state they are left day after day, a nuisance to passengers, without the least notice being taken of them, by those whose duty it is to guard the public from injury.

About the middle of the sixteenth century, the then existing Corporation granted an exclusive privilege to certain undertakers, as they are styled in the lease, to erect an engine, whereby to supply the inhabitants with water, from the river Kennet, for the term of one thousand years: but it does not appear, that they themselves were invested with any such authority, by their Charter; it is in fact a monopoly; and all monopolies were, I believe, declared to be illegal, by the House of Commons, in the reign of Charles I; nay, they even obliged that Monarch to recall the patents he had granted

all monopolies: Charles, like previous monarchs, readily granted monopolies to courtiers as rewards; the Long Parliament's attempt to abolish the system was hardly effective.

to several individuals, as well as companies, for an exclusive privilege of carrying on certain trades. If I am correct, in this statement, the exclusive right granted by the Corporation, cannot be valid against any other company, who may hereafter undertake to supply the town, from this or any other source, on equal, or better terms, and with more punctuality. I was induced to make these observations, from the general discontent expressed by those I conversed with on the subject, from their not being regularly supplied with water, as they had a right to expect. On enquiry, I found this was owing to the injudicious construction of the engine, and the badness of the pipes; the *mechanical power* of the *former* being to the resistance of the latter nearly as *ten* to *one*; add to this, that in the same range, pipes were laid down of all bores, from two inches and a half diameter to six; the consequence of this was, that as the smaller bores became choaked, the water was forced back on the engine, 'till either that, or the pipes, gave way; if the former, it took a long time to repair it; and, if the latter, the streets were deluged with water, which was sometimes suffered to stagnate for months. A friend of mine, who is a great fisherman, seeing a large pond in the street, before a fishmonger's shop, mistook it for a *reservoir* for his fish, and actually asked his permission *to throw a line* in it.

Such, I am informed, has been the state of the town, from the bursting of the pipes, for many years past, but I understand, that a new set of proprietors have undertaken to conduct the works, on better principles; and, as far as I can judge, from what they have hitherto done, have shewn a great deal of skill and ingenuity in the improvements they have adopted; their expences in consequence must be great; yet there can be no doubt, but those who are benefitted by their exertions, will cheerfully contribute towards their reimbursement.

These water-works are a great benefit to the town, not only by supplying the inhabitants with water for culinary purposes, but as they are a security against fire; now rendered the more necessary on account of all the former dipping-places, on the Kennet and neighbouring brooks, having been closed up, by the modern improvements the town has undergone. But it is evident, that this cannot, at all times, be relied on, as either frost or floods are liable to put a stop to the operation of the machine; in either case, should a fire happen, the greater part of the town, but particularly the Market-place, having only the wells to depend on, which are soon exhausted, might be endangered, for want of a sufficient supply of water to keep the engines in full play. This inconvenience, I think, might be remedied, at an easy expence. There is a perennial spring, of fine water, belonging to the Corporation, called the Conduit, from its having formerly supplied the Abbey with a purer element than that afforded by the river. It is situated on a hill of sufficient elevation to be capable, by its own gravity, of being conveyed by pipes to the highest part of the town, without the assistance of mechanical powers. Had the worthy gentleman, I mentioned in my former letter, who erected the lamp-post in the Market-place, converted it into a fountain, for the benefit of the neighbourhood, it might have been of incalculable service. To do this, nothing more was wanting, than to have formed the base into a large bason, supplied with cocks at the facets of the three angles, and covered over with a handsome cupola, whereon the shaft might have been erected as it now is, with its accompanying lamp-irons: the whole additional

the Conduit: Very little evidence has been found to prove that Whitley Conduit supplied the Abbey, which had its own well and the Holy Brook to drink from.

lamp-post: the Simeon monument, see p.19.

expence would have been in the leaden pipe to convey the water; but, as this would not have required a great bore, perhaps two hundred pounds would have been sufficient to have completed this truly desirable object.

Among the nuisances that embarrass the passages of this populous town, may be reckoned *umbrellas*; these are now used by every class, from the peer, the parson, or the magistrate, down to the porter or the pot-girl. For this reason, I seldom go out on a wet day; there being then no passing these formidable barriers without being *blessed* with a pailfull of water down your back, or having one of *your eyes* thrust out with the brass ends of the ribs, extending, for this express purpose, two inches beyond the silk covering. Heavens! what have I not undergone, when overtaken by a shower? I have found my steps retarded, or my way obstructed, by some diminutive old hag, with an *enormous umbrella* over her head, extending more than a yard beyond the foot-path, precluding passengers from all possibility of passing in a direct line: thus situated, I have sometimes been obliged to precipitate myself into the high-way, at the expence perhaps of a clean pair of white stockings, and when I had recovered my former track, have been again and again thrust out of my course, by a whole row of *land tortoises*, of the same description, who seemed to have conspired to *drown* one half of the people they *met*, and to make those *behind* them run mad. It is for this reason, I suppose, that every one here wears *boots*; it being as uncommon to see *a tailor's apprentice* without them, as a *shoe-black* without an *umbrella*; a custom that might induce a stranger to suppose, that every one he met was going to *take horse*, when perhaps he was only in search of *a leg of mutton,* or *a bunch of*

turnips, for dinner. As to the ladies, you know, they are always ready to meet the gentlemen *half way;* it cannot therefore be surprising, if, following the fashion, they also have adopted *half boots*.

While speaking of the ladies, I cannot help noticing a custom assumed by the pretty misses of this place, of walking,

three or four together, *arm in arm*, but so intent in conversation, or so wrapt up in the contemplation of their own dear selves, that they seem incapable of distinguishing any other objects about them; thus the blind, the lame, and the halt, the aged and infirm, are obliged to *give way* to these *impenetrable* phalanxes; it is in vain the passenger endeavors to slip by them, by taking the wall or the gutter, for like *good generals,* they are always on the watch, to prevent the enemy *turning their flanks.* If he happen to be in their *rear*, he has no alternative but crossing to the other side of the way; and if he should be so unfortunate as to come up with their *van,* he stands a very good chance of being upset, or thrown off his basis; for the dear creatures never give *any quarter.* I was a long time puzzled how to act upon these occasions; at length I hit upon the following *ruse de guerre,* which has answered beyond my most sanguine expectations: pretending to be as absent from thought as themselves, I take care to dodge one of them, just as you have seen people do who have met in a hurry, now backwards, now forwards, now they fly to the right, now to the left, always taking the same direction, till they either come in *contact* with each other, or one of the parties makes a full stand, for the benefit of both. By this manœuvre, I generally succeed in *breaking their line,* though I have never yet been able to *disperse them* altogether, or *to put them out of countenance.*

Would it not be more becoming in such young ladies, and a greater proof of their good sense, if they were sometimes to give way to the urgency of other people's affairs; and, upon all occasions, to remember, that the *meanest individual* has as much right to pass in the open streets, without interruption, as themselves?

There is one more *nuisance* in this town, which I must mention, tho' with regret, as it concerns one of the simplest but best characters in it: This is a poor industrious fellow, who traverses the streets from morning 'till night, with a large basket on each arm, filled with cakes and other *rarities* for children; continually calling out *Nice new! nice new!* With sometimes the gratifying addition of----*Here they be! two sizes bigger than last week!* in a melancholy tone of voice, sufficient to unstring the nerves, and damp the vivacity of a

French dancing master. This poor fellow, with his baskets, so completely blocks up the way, wherever you chance to meet him, that, however great your hurry, your passage is for a while interrupted; and yet, upon such occasions, so great has been my respect for his character, for industry, honesty, and his affectionate regard for some near female relatives; to make a small provision for whom, he is said nearly to starve himself, that I have, every time we met, almost involuntarily put my hand to my hat, to pay him that compliment, which custom has taught us to pay to our *superiors*. In consonance with the simplicity and goodness of his heart, he has been perverted to methodism, and has the honor to blow the bellows for the chapel organ. On one of these occasions, happening to fall a-sleep in his seat, during the *sermon*, which he did not very well comprehend, and dreaming he was traversing the streets with his baskets, he all at once broke out in his usual tone *All hot! all hot!* to the great entertainment of the congregation, who, notwithstanding the solemnity of the occasion, could not help *smiling* at the abruptness of the interruption.

This town has, at all times, been famous for odd characters, who, from their peculiarities, have attracted the notice of the public; among those, of the present day, may be reckoned *Milk below, Maids!* This person, like *Nice new!* has many excentricities in his manner, but not one that impeaches his character: he is sober, honest, and industrious, and therefore a better member of society than many that pride themselves on belonging to a higher rank. Whether his excentricities are natural or assumed, I cannot take upon myself to say, but they are certainly inoffensive. At times he employs himself in hawking fish about, and during the winter season, you may hear his

Milk below: W S Darter tells us that this character's name was Russ, and that he died worth £300.

melodious cry of *Periwinks! periwinks!* in every street, accompanied with the trilling blast of his *horn*, which he is never without: at other seasons he runs of errands, or cries milk, at *any time of the day* but the usual one, when his horn is of great use in calling out the *Naiads* and *Goddesses of the Kitchen!* In all these occupations, and whatever may be the season of the year, he is uncoated, if I may be allowed the expression; his waistcoat is tied behind with a number of ribbons of various colors; his hat is covered with a profusion of flowers; and he has generally a large *bouquet* in his bosom, big enough for *a stable broom*, composed of ever-greens, sun-flowers, and flowers of all descriptions; in the winter season, he is dressed like our *churches,* in *yew* and *holly!* and might easily be taken for an Indian Chief!-----With all this oddity about him, I respect his character, and heartily wish, that this place afforded no worse members of society.

Considering the number of schemes, that have, within the last twenty years, been *talked of,* for the improvement of the town, or the advantage of its inhabitants, I am surprised at not finding a local insurance office established among them, though notices of all the London offices are displayed, either in large gilt letters in the windows, or by some device over the door, in almost every street in the town: this, to an observing mind, one would think, must point out a certain source of profit, within the reach of every monied man, but which no one has hitherto had courage or ability to grasp. The advantage derived to this place, from a large river, and several brooks, running through it in different directions, is so great, that, in case of an accident by fire, it is very soon extinguished, an ample supply of water being always at hand to keep the

Indeed I have heard: as Secretary to the Reading Provident Society for eight years or more, Man had some experience of the insurance business; his son Horace was an agent for the Globe.

engines at work, (except in times of frost or floods) from one or other of these sources. Indeed I have heard, from good authority, that the *annual* revenue paid to the London offices, from this town, is more than sufficient to make good all the losses it has experienced from fire for the last *fifty years*. Now let us suppose, that the town had paid for insurances only one hundred pounds a year; this, in fifty years, without reckoning the interest, would amount to five thousand pounds, and taking the average loss, in the whole fifty years, according to the above statement, at one year's purchase, or one hundred pounds, we shall find the loss incurred by the town, from this oversight, to be, *four thousand nine hundred pounds!*

and so in proportion for every hundred pounds laid out. It is strange therefore, with these facts before their eyes, that none of the great capitalists here, have set on foot an office of this kind; perhaps this can only be accounted for, by imputing it to that jealousy among individuals, so common in country towns; where each, wishing to draw the whole emolument to himself, had rather see any scheme fail, however lucrative it might be, than his neighbour should share with him in it. But an insurance office ought not to be established for the enriching of a few individuals only; if it should, the inhabitants at large might as well continue with the old ones; as it must be of no moment to them, whether individuals, in another place, or here, should alone reap the benefit. Let every insurer partake both of the risk and the profit, and I am convinced an office might easily be established here, that would very soon supersede all the others.

There has lately been erected here, a neat little Theatre, where a very respectable company perform, (I had almost said to empty benches,) for a few weeks in autumn; but certain it is, they meet with very little encouragement from the inhabitants: this is partly owing to the bigotry of the methodists; and in part to the immoderate thirst for gain, that pervades every class of shop-keepers, making them regret the loss of every shilling, that, by any other means, is prevented from finding its way to their tills. Thus the sons of *Thespis* are almost banished from a town, whose inhabitants might certainly benefit from their exhibitions, if they were properly encouraged here, as they are among the most polished nations of Europe. It is well known, that theatrical exhibitions were encouraged in all the republics of ancient Greece; and even

a neat little Theatre: Henry Thornton had opened the town's first purpose-built theatre in Friar Street in 1788; it was the fifth in what was to become a circuit of more than 20. Thornton was evidently concerned that Man's comments might harm his trade, and persuaded the *Mercury* to print, on 10 September 1810, the following: 'We trust that this deserving company will meet with such support from the enlightened inhabitants of this town and neighbourhood, as completely to wipe off the stigma which has been thrown upon it in a recent publication…'

the more austere inhabitants of Rome were indebted to them for a great part of their morality and civilization; but, in this *enlightened* town, they are not only received with disgust, and treated with neglect, but the people are instructed, from the pulpit, to consider them as dangerous to religion, and engines of the *Tempter* to seduce them from their religious duties. Thus, after casting a dimness over their own sight, their preachers endeavor to prevent their hearers benefiting by the light of others, whose creed may be equally orthodox, though somewhat more enlightened. I would not have you, however, infer from this, that the generality of tradesmen here have no *taste;* far from it, all I mean to say is, that they display much more in decorating their shops, than in improving their minds, by participating in theatrical amusements. It is probable they have been encouraged to pursue this line of conduct, by the advantages they derive from their local situation, between two rivers, which, uniting with many of the canals, already finished, in the western division of the kingdom, enables them to supply, not only the inhabitants of the borough, but also those of the neighbouring towns, and villages, for many miles round, with every article of colonial consumption, and home manufactures, on equal terms with those of the capital. Thus many of them grow rich, by persevering industry, who can scarce write their names; and, by their success, give encouragement to those, who succeed them, to follow the same track. Another advantage they derive, is from the numerous stage-coaches that pass through the town, almost every hour in the day: an accommodation that enables the tradesman here, who leaves his home in the morning, to transact what business he may have to do in London, and to return the same evening. This facility of travelling, and the ready communication with the capital, encourages many respectable private families to reside here, in preference to other places: to this choice, however, they have other inducements; among these may be reckoned, the cheapness and regularity of the markets, which are profusely supplied with every article the choicest voluptuary can require; for, though this is an inland town, fish may be had every day by two o'clock, fresh from Billingsgate market. The bread also is the finest and whitest in the kingdom, as well as the best tasted, if eaten within four and twenty hours after it has been baked; but after that time, it is harsh, dry, and unpleasant to the taste: whether this be owing to *the nature of the grain,* from which it is made, or the *want of a sufficient quantity of alum* in the mixture, is not for me to determine. Though I cannot say much in praise of their beer, I think it is *as good* as the most skilful *modern chymist* could brew without *malt* or *hops*. To these substantial allurements, may be added a variety of amusements, that are to be found here. I have already mentioned the Theatre; to this may be added, horse-races, reviews, balls, assemblies, coteries, card-parties, and concerts, for the ladies; fishing, hunting, coursing, and shooting, for the gentlemen; for, notwithstanding the *insulting* prohibitory mandates of almost every petty lord of a manor, exhibited in the newspapers previous to the shooting season, the gun still follows with impunity, where the dogs lead. Were I a lord of a manor, and wanted to preserve my game, instead of forbidding, I would invite, all sportsmen to shoot on it, that wished to do so; because, if I know the disposition of my country-men, I am convinced that every true sportsman would use

the most skilful *modern chymist*: This pre-CAMRA complaint is not necessarily directed at Simonds; there were several other brewers in town. They allegedly operated a cartel, keeping prices up and quality down because the magistrates would not issue enough licences. In 2005 we complain that there are too many boozers…

horse-races: Bulmershe Heath was the racecourse. Miss Mitford called it 'a dull, flat, low, unprofitable piece of ground'.

the indulgence with moderation, because he would feel it an obligation; while, on the contrary, he would do his utmost to destroy the game on *forbidden* ground, because he would feel it *a duty* to resist the assumption of such arbitrary power: from those who were not real sportsmen, I should have nothing to fear, because their want of skill, by rendering the birds shy, would be one of the best means of preserving them.

I had almost forgot to mention the dispensary, lately established here, by voluntary subscription; attended, in rotation, by the physicians and apothecaries, gratis. This is one of those modern charities, which this nation abounds with, more specious in appearance, than effectual in its consequences. It is, I believe, still problematical, whether the science of medicine has been beneficial, or detrimental, to the human race? Were the professors of this art, to confine their practice to a few simple, and known cases, and apply for their cure, such medicines only, as have been proved efficacious, I have no doubt but great benefits might be derived from them; but when the gentlemen of the faculty presume to prescribe various and discordant drugs, in the cure of diseases, originating from causes, which, with all their skill, they have been unable to discover, then it is, that medicine, instead of being a relief to the patient, becomes his distruction. How far this establishment may answer the benefits expected to be derived from it, I cannot say; but, if we may judge from the last annual return of the managers, the good derived from it, was not inconsiderable. From this statement, it appears, that 409 patients have, in the course of the year, been supplied with *medicines,* and advice, *gratis*; of these, 305 had been *cured*, 45 were still on the list, and the rest, as might have been expected, had either *died* or *ran away*! But, what appears to me, most extraordinary in this statement, is the *number* of *poor* patients, in such an *opulent* place as this, and where more than 300 of the poorest are provided for in the parish-workhouses, and consequently can have no claim to relief from the dispensary. If we take the population of the town at 10,000, and allow one-fourth, or 2,500 for the indigent, which is a very great proportion, and deduct from it 500, for such as are otherwise provided for, the remainder will be 2000; this, divided by 409, (the number it appears applied for relief,) will give nearly *one in five* sick, in this discription of persons, at a time when no epidemical disorders prevailed, and when the other classes seem to have been unusually free from disease. At first, I was very much surprised to find, that so many of my fellow-creatures had gone through a *regular course* of physic with *impunity,* 'till, having recourse to calculation, I found, that the quantity of drugs dispensed to each patient, did not cost quite *three shillings;* a sum totally inadequate to produce that *mortality,* which would have *followed,* among an equal number of richer patients, who could have *afforded to die* secundum artem.---*What a blessing is poverty!*

At my first arrival, I had some difficulty in understanding the natives; as they use a *jargon* not very harmonious, or grammatical. Like their ancestors, the Danes and Saxons, they still retain the plural *en,* in many words, as hous*en,* hors*en,* ho-s*en,* except oxen, for which they use ox*es.* Their nouns have only two genders, the masculine, and feminine: these serve for all purposes, but the former is most in use. The personal pronoun *him,* contracted into *in,* serves, when joined to the foregoing word, to express every thing, whether animate, or

At my first arrival: A modern traveller would be hard put to tell from the inhabitants' speech what part of the country she had reached; Estuary English rules. A few of the oldest generation still sport a Berkshire burr, and pronounce 'town' as 'tane'; the youthful rendering of 'home' as 'hame' has more to do with Australian soap operas.

45

inanimate, *male,* or *female;* thus, if I ask for the paper, the waiter will perhaps tell me, "A gem'man has gott'*in* in hand, but he'll bring'*in* when he's done with'*in;*" I one day heard a lady call to her little boy, "Take care of that *cow,* Billey, *he'*ll butt you with *his* horns." As to their verbs, they so confuse the *moods, tenses,* and *numbers,* as to render it impossible for the best philologist to comprehend their meaning. In most other places, two negatives make an affirmative: but this is not the case here; where you will frequently hear such sentences as, *I never did nothing to offend him; I do'nt know nothing about it;* however, by reversing the idea, as the eye is said to do objects in vision, and supposing them to *intend just the reverse of what they say,* I often catch their true meaning.

There is one remark a *Stranger* cannot fail to make in this place; and that is, the number of bald-headed people he is in the daily habit of seeing: at first, I thought this phenomenon might be owing to their well-water, which is strongly impregnated with the sulphate of lime; but I have since altered that opinion, on observing that many of these smooth headed people have an utter aversion to that element: never suffering it to come within their lips. Some people think it is owing to the *heat* of the *brain,* which drys up all the pores intended for the nourishment of the hair, that vegetable ornament of the human head; but this I can by no means admit, as I have met with some instances, where it was evident the patient never possessed any *brains* at all; I must, therefore, leave this question, for the present, undetermined, but not without hopes, that the medical staff here, which is *sufficiently numerous* for all *good* purposes, will, on some future day, give us a solution that may be depended upon.

sulphate of lime: calcium sulphate would commonly occur in well waters and is a cause of 'permanent hardness' – that is, it is not destroyed by boiling, unlike calcium bicarbonate. There is no evidence that it causes or speeds balding, but it is alleged to be good for brewing; notably, it is strongly present in Burton-on-Trent.

I was going to congratulate the town on having all at once got rid of their attornies, 'till I found, strange to tell, that the *name* only, and not their *profession* had been changed: those, who were before attornies, being now solicitors: a change, however, that carries with it some propriety; as under the name of attornies, nobody knew what they were, or what the word meant, 'till they *felt it*. Bailey says, it is derived from *ad,* Latin, and *tour,* French, and that it signifies, *every man in his turn;* but the attorney first, as is most natural! Under the word, *solicitor,* however, which they have adopted, there can be no doubt but they mean to be *solicitous,* either for the *good* of their *clients* or *themselves;* but which will have the preference we must leave to posterity to determine.

It is surprising, that in so *high spirited* a town as this, the system of *begging* should be universally practised among the lower orders. If you *ask* one of these *the time of the day,* you are immediately called upon for *charity*; if you have to *walk through a gateway,* children are planted at it to ask *charity;* and every one you meet in the dress of poverty, asks *charity,* though they are, or have a right to be, amply provided for by their parishes; but this contemptible, degrading spirit, is not confined to *real* paupers: men who can earn from 20 to 30 shillings a week wages, are not only, not above asking for *drink money,* every day they are employed, but even look upon it as their right, and will resent it, if their demand be not complied with, by trifling away that time, which is not properly their own, but their employers: and thus adding *dishonesty* to *imposition.* I have heard, that in Italy, where the poor work for a *julio* (sixpence) a day, they never beg, and even resent it as an *affront* when charity is offered them; and yet my high-spirited

got rid of their attornies: Man's surprise at the change of professional name is surprising. The word 'solicitor' was well established and virtually synonymous with 'attorney' by 1810; but adverts in the *Mercury* show that Reading was only catching on in 1806. Pigot's directory (1830) still uses the older title exclusively.

system of *begging*: Since the reign of Margaret Thatcher, begging has again become a fact of Reading life.

countrymen, who have ten times that sum, are so lost to all
sense of decent pride, as to become almost common beggars,
without blushing at their own baseness of spirit.

In the above picture of the town, and its inhabitants, I am
fearful you will accuse me of *partiality;* but, I can assure you,
it is drawn from the life; and if it should afford you any entertainment, it will be a sufficient recompence for the time
bestowed upon it, by

Your's, &c. &c.
Reading, ----------------

LETTER 4
some famous Readingensians, *and literary life*

To ⸺⸺⸺⸺

In compliance with the wish you expressed in your last, that I would give you some account of the progress, and present state, of literature, in this town, I have now the pleasure of sending you such information as I have been able to collect, either from reading, or conversation with the inhabitants. I could have wished that it had been more full and satisfactory than it is; for, unless I have overlooked in it, as is very probably the case, many respectable writers, and learned natives, of the town, you will conclude, that the *soil* of Reading has not been very productive of men of genius, and that the few names here recorded, have added very little to the general stock of the literature of the country. In the early period of our history, down to the introduction of printing, every species of learning was almost exclusively confined to the secular and regular clergy: it is therefore among these only, that we can expect to find the subjects of our present enquiry, to that period. But of these, I have only discovered three or four.

The first upon record, is Robert de Radynge, who probably took his surname from his native town, as was common, among learned men, in those days. He was prior of Leominster, a cell to the Abbey of Reading, to which he was promoted by the abbot, he being one of the monks belonging to the monas-

In the early period: Like the first edition of the *DNB*, Man's list is over-stuffed with unremembered clerics.

Robert de Radynge: The Chronicon Roberti de Redyng is a monk's account of English history from 1299–1325. He was said to have been one of only two Englishmen who understood Arabic in the reign of Henry I.

49

Robert Grosstête: Grosseteste (c.1170–1253) was a polymath of 'torrential energy' (*DNB*); he wrote *On the Calendar, On the Movement of the Planets, On the Origin of Sounds* and *On Light*. He came from a poor family in Suffolk, and happened to be consecrated as Bishop of Lincoln in Reading Abbey in 1235. Upon this tenuous connexion Man hangs his feeble pun insulting his fellow townsmen.

John Blagrave: Blagrave was indeed a native.

tery from whence most of the priors were taken. All we know of him further is, that he was a great mathematician, and died in 1190.

The next was, Robert Grosstête, (Anglice *Thick-head**) Bishop of Lincoln, who was consecrated here in 1235; but we have no account of his writings: only he is said to have been a very learned man.

Robert Mason, born at Reading, was educated at Oxford, where he took the degree of Doctor in Civil Law. He was afterwards archdeacon of Northumberland, and precentor of Lincoln. His writings have probably long since perished. He died in 1493.

Mr. John Blagrave was a very eminent mathematician, as appears from his numerous publications. He resided here the greater part of his life; but whether he was a native, or born at one of the family seats in the neighbourhood, is uncertain: he died in 1611, and was buried in St. Lawrence's church, under a monument erected in conformity with the instructions given in his will.

Nathaniel Canon, a native, was born in the sixteenth century: he was vicar of Hurley, and published some sermons, which are now probably lost. He died in 1664.

Mr. Thomas Turner was educated at the free school at Reading; from whence he went to St. John's College in Oxford. He was patronised by Archbishop Laud, by whose interest he became successively chaplain in ordinary to Charles I. canon residentiary of St. Paul's, and ninth dean of Canterbury. On

---

* This family must have been originally numerous, as many of their descendents are still to be found in various parts of the town.   EDITOR.

the breaking out of the civil war, he was sequestered from his livings, and obliged to conceal himself from his enemies. Charles II. restored him to all his dignities; but these he did not long enjoy, dying in 1672, and was buried in Canterbury Cathedral. If the following lines on his father's tombstone were written by this gentleman, they afford but an indifferent specimen of his abilities as a writer, at least as a poet:

Fourscore I lived, four stemns I leave *behinde,*
Four times of Readinge maioraltie *sustained.*
My soule in Christ's hand I have *resigned,*
And here my corpes interred do *remaine.*
The grave her due, his tribute death requires,
Happy is he whose soule to heaven aspires.

He left behind him three sons; one of which, Dr. T. Turner, was archdeacon of Essex, president of C. C. College, Oxford, precentor of St. Paul's Cathedral, and chaplain in ordinary to Charles II. he died April 30, 1714, and was buried in the chapel of his college, where there is a long inscription to his memory. He was a most munificent benefactor to the society for the relief of the widows and orphans of the established clergy: to which he bequeathed the sum of 20,000l. With this sum, the trustees purchased an estate at Stow-Nine-Churches, in Northamptonshire, where a monument was erected to his memory, a print of which has been engraved by Sturt.

William, the second son, was D.D. archdeacon of Northumberland, and died in 1685.

Dr. Francis Turner, the other brother, past in regular succession through the whole course of *ecclesiastical preferment:* He was fellow of New College, in Oxford, and master of St. John's; rector of Tharfield, a prebendary of St. Paul's, dean of Windsor, bishop of Rochester, and lastly, Bishop of Ely; all of which he forfeited at the revolution, by refusing to take the oaths to William III. He died in 1700, and was buried in a humble manner at Tharfield.

It is very probable that these three divines might not be natives of Reading, though their father was; however, I mention them here, to shew you, how far even a small portion of *Reading blood* may advance those in life, who know how to use it with *discretion.*

Archbishop Laud was undoubtedly born here, and as he says, of honest and industrious parents in the clothing line.* He was educated at the free-school, and sent on Sir Thomas Whyte's foundation, to St. John's College, Oxon. He is considered by some here, as the pride and boast of the town, but in this I must differ from them. If we trace his path through

Laud: An anonymous tract of 1691 ingeniously reads the letters WILL LAUD as Roman numerals and adds them up: ignoring the A and treating the U as a V and the W as two Vs, you get the alarming total of 666. QED.

life, we shall find him the greatest sycophant perhaps that ever lived: To those from whom he expected preferment he was all obsequiousness and submission; while, to those who opposed his measures, he was haughty, brutal, and vindictive. That he was cruel by nature, cannot be doubted, he having left too many instances on record to prove it. When Felton was examined before the High Court of Starchamber, for the murder of Laud's patron, the Duke of Buckingham, the bishop said: "if you will not confess you must *go to the rack.*" to which the prisoner replied, "If it must be so, I know not, whom I may accuse in the extremity of the torture: *Bishop Laud perhaps, or any Lord at the Board.*" Sound sense, says Judge Foster, in the mouth of an enthusiast.----By his flattery to the great, he rose to the highest dignity in the church, which he nearly ruined by his bigotry and inhumanity towards the dissenters. To the arbitrary and unconstitutional principles he is supposed to have instilled into the mind of his unfortunate Sovereign, may be imputed all the troubles that subsequently disturbed the kingdom for so many years, and at length brought them both to an untimely end on the scaffold.

Laud was rather a patron of learning and learned men, than a great scholar. To the University of Oxford he presented 1400 MSS. in various languages, as well as a collection of ancient coins, and gave them part of his estate at Bray to establish an

---

* Hee was borne at *Redding* in *Barkshire: Octob.* 7. 1573. of poore and obscure Parents, in a Cottage, just over against the Cage: which Cage since his comming to the Archbishoprick of *Canterbury*, upon complaint of Master *Elveston* (that it was a dishonour the Cage should be suffered to stand so neare the House, where so great a Royall Favourite, and Prelate had his birth) was removed to some other place; and the Cottage pulled downe, and new built by the Bishop.　Prynne's Breviate

Arabic professorship; but it does not appear, that he wrote any thing considerable himself, except his reply to Fisher, the Jesuite, and a few sermons. Perhaps his *will* was the best thing he ever wrote, as far as it regards his native town; wherein he confirmed his former gift to the Corporation, of the remaining part of his estate and manor, at Bray, to the value of 200l. per annum, in trust for the benefit of the poor;* and appointed the heads of St. John's College triennial visitors, to see that the Corporation *properly* executed the trust committed to their management. On these occasions, the heads of the college are entertained by the Corporation; when we may suppose the accounts are *regularly examined* and *passed*; and as it does not appear that any *objections* have, at any time, been made by the visitors, to their management of the charity, we may, I think, conclude, that it has always been administered with the *greatest integrity, according to the will of the donor.*

The next writer on record was Mr. Joseph Blagrave, who seems, from the works he published, to have been an apothecary, they being chiefly on drugs, and the efficacy of herbs in curing all kinds of diseases: but his principal work was, his Introduction to Astrology, a science closely connected, in

---

* *In Abp. Laud's Diary, written by himself, are the following Entries:*

To settle an *Hospitall* of Land in *Redding* of 100 pounds a yeare in a new way. I have acquainted Mr. *Barnard* the Vicar of *Croyden* with my project. He is to call upon my Executors to do it, if the surplusage of my goods after debts and Charges paid, come to 3000 pounds. *Done to the value of* 200 pounds *per Annum.*

To erect an *Arabicke* Lecture in *Oxford,* at least for my life time, my state not being able for more: that this may lead the way, &c. The Lecture began to be read, *August* 10. 1636. *Done.* I have now setled it for ever.

Editor.

those days, with the *art of healing*, as it is improperly called; in which, if not an adept, he was certainly an enthusiast. ------This is the only *conjuror*, I believe, that was ever *born in Reading*. He died in 1679.

William Creed was a divine of some note, in the seventeenth century. He is said "to have been a zealous defender of the Church of England in the worst of times:"* but this character does not coincide with his conduct, during the *usurpation,* when he was promoted to, and suffered to enjoy, the living of East Codford, Wilts.------Perhaps, living so nigh, he might have heard of the *Vicar of Bray*.

Christopher Cheesman, one of those people improperly called Quakers, was a native of Reading. He was living at the restoration of Charles II. about which time he published a pamphlet at London, with the following title: "An Epistle to Charles II. and to every individual Member of the Counsel. Presented to them in pure love, and good will, that they might consider of the things, herein contained, before the King was crowned, or had taken his oath, forasmuch as a *necessity from the Lord was laid upon the penman*, of the said epistle, in order thereto; who is known to divers people by the name of Christopher Cheesman, from the town of Reading, in Berkshire, the 15th of the second month, 1661."------As Quakerism took its rise about this period, it is probable that Mr. Cheesman was one of its earliest converts, and, as such, bore a great part in the persecutions these inoffensive people underwent, for the conscientious resistance to the laws in force against them; particularly the one for preventing

Vicar of Bray: The Vicar who famously changed his views to keep his job was probably Simon Aleyn, who survived through the reigns of Henry VIII, Edward VI, Mary and Elizabeth, though the popular song shifts him to a later period.

---

* Mr. Coates' History.

55

religious meetings in conventicles, and private houses, and that, which was enacted during this reign, whereby all his Majesty's subjects were obliged to take the oath of allegiance, when called upon by the magistrates; in default whereof, they were, for the first offence, to be imprisoned, at the discretion of the judges; for the second offence, they incurred a premunire, whereby their real estates were forfeited during their lives, and their personal for ever; and, for the third, they were to be transported for seven years, to any of his Majesty's West India Islands.

By virtue of these acts, the Quakers were persecuted with the utmost rigor: they were imprisoned, plundered, and transported from every town in the country, but more particularly from corporations, where the magistrates were more under the influence of the ruling powers. Accordingly we find, they were, for many years, treated with all the rigor of the laws, in this town; but their sufferings appear to have risen to the highest pitch in this reign, about the time of Mr. George Thorne's mayoralty, whom the Quakers called, "*A great Persecutor of the Saints*," and apparently not without reason, for, in January 1660, he went, attended by his constables, to the meeting, and took out this Mr. Cheesman, and ten others, men and women, and committed them to the counter; and in July following, he, with Mr. Alderman Sikes, and Mr. Hugh Smith, the town clerk, attended as before, again broke up the meeting, and committed Mr. Cheesman and *forty-five* others to bridewell, for refusing to take the oath of allegiance; where they remained 'till the next quarter sessions, when they were tried for this offence, and for being at an unlawful meeting; and on their refusing to give security for their good behavior, were re-committed to prison, where they remained 'till the following April. This severity, used to a set of inoffensive people, for holding a few speculative tenets contrary to the established church, might be supposed sufficient to have damped the ardor of the most enthusiastic among them; but this was not the case: if they were turned out of the meeting to-day, they returned to it to-morrow; and, if the doors were

shut against them, they held their meetings in the street, even during the severest weather: In conformity with this practice, tho' Mr. Cheesman had undergone a severe imprisonment of several months within the space of one year: he was no sooner set at liberty than he returned regularly to the meeting, where he, and six women, being again taken, were carried before Mr. Sikes, then mayor, who, from lenity, fined them only one shilling each, the penalty for not being at church; but, on their refusing to pay the fine, he was under the necessity of committing them again to bridewell, from whence, however, they were the next day discharged. This occurrence took place in 1664, and a few days after, being again found preaching in the meeting, he was taken from thence, with nine of his brethren, who were all committed to prison, to take their trials, at the next sessions; when this being considered the third offence against the laws, committed by Mr. Cheesman, and aggravated, as it was alleged, by his carrying letters about the country, to confirm his afflicted brethren, he would have been transported, had not the grand jury, through compassion, as it is said, thrown out the bill: however, as he refused to pay the fees, he was remanded back to prison, as a *factious* person!

Tantum Religio: 'So much evil could religion persuade people to perform' (Lucretius).

"Tantum Religio potuit suadere malorum."

What became of him afterwards, I have not been able to learn; but every man's feelings must be shocked at the cruelty offered to these harmless people, for exercising their right to choose their own religion: a right, that every other religious sect has at times claimed, though with the strangest inconsistency; when in power, everyone has shewn a disposition to curb it in others.

Rev. James Merrick, B.A. was the son of a physician, who resided in this town, and a member of the Corporation. He was certainly the most learned divine that Reading ever gave birth to. His works are numerous, and have all a tendency to instruct or improve mankind. As a furtherance to the knowledge of the Greek language, he engaged many of the town's boys educating in the free-school, to make Greek indexes, some of which were afterwards published. He wrote many poetical works of great merit: but his translation of the psalms is what finally stamped his character as a fine writer. He died in 1769, after a short illness, either broken hearted or insane, perhaps both; owing to the anguish of mind, occasioned by a most *infamous* and wicked imputation cast upon him by his own footman, and too lightly believed by his friends, most of whom henceforth shunned his acquaintance: a shock, his sensibility could not long survive.

Mr. R. Cole, commonly called Poet Cole, to distinguish him from a *little* gentleman of the same name, who, for the like reason was called *Small Cole,* was a native of Reading, where he constantly resided on the income of a small estate, which came to him by inheritance. Having never been engaged in business, he was induced, for want of employment, to spend more of his time at clubs and public-houses than was consistent with strict propriety, tho' sanctioned by the general practice of his neighbours. It was observed on these occasions, that he was the last to leave these convivial meetings, always staying as long as he could prevail on anyone of the party to keep him company, even at the expence of his pocket, and when this allurement failed, he has been known to remain at his post 'till the servant came to prepare the room for the next

James Merrick: Merrick, born in 1720, published a tract at the age of 14. A biblical and classical scholar and translator, he retired to his home town and took a great interest in the welfare of its prisoners.

day, and yet he was never known to be intoxicated: probably, when left to himself on these occasions, he might be meditating on some expression, or some trait in the characters of his companions, which might find employment for his pen on the succeeding day. It is a pity that his poems were not collected into a volume, many of them being as creditable to his head as his heart; but wanting due encouragement from his brother townsmen, they only occasionally made their appearance in the Reading Mercury, and were forgot. He died in the year 1777.

The last writer, of note, that I have met with, was, Mr. William Baker, a printer, in London: he received his education in his native town, under his father, and, by his application to study, obtained a knowledge of the Greek, Latin, French, and Italian languages: he wrote a small work called "The Rationalist" in which there were some dissertations that shewed a thinking mind. He also published a selection from the Greek and Latin writers, and several minor pieces. He died in 1785.

It is rather surprising, that this town should have produced so few learned men, considering the advantages the inhabitants possessed, of having their children educated at the *Free*-grammar school, formerly *free* of all costs, as its name implies: In process of time, from the generosity of the parents, it became customary to make the master a present at Christmas; this was soon converted into a fixed quarter-age; and, at present, if I am informed right, it has so much deviated from its original foundation, as to have become a seminary for gentlemen's sons only, who have no connection with the town; while the natives, for whose benefit alone it was instituted, are obliged to seek their education elsewhere:

William Baker: Man's brother-in-law: see introduction.

.

but the mischief does not end here, for the two scholarships to St. John's College, Oxford, given to the town by Sir Thos. Whyte, for the encouragement of the scholars, are in danger of being lost; it being evident, if none but strangers are to be educated in the school, no others can be competent, according to the statutes, to be elected; and thus will this great benefit be lost to the natives, unless the Corporation, at the next vacancy, should call it back to its old foundation, and suffer none but *natives* to be educated within its walls: and this they are better able to do at this, than at any former period, as an excellent house has lately been purchased, for the master, by subscription, in addition, I believe, to an adequate stipend for the discharge of his duty, given by Archbishop Laud.

If this town produced so few learned men, while the inhabitants were in the undiminished enjoyment of their right to give their children a classical education at a small, if any expence, it is much to be apprehended, that it will not be more productive in future, when this invaluable advantage shall be lost.-----It is not the selling a loaf of bread, or a joint of meat more, that can compensate the town for this sacrifice of one of its dearest rights: unless the mind be informed by erudition, the gold of the possessor has lost more than half its value; and unless the lower classes are enlightened by education, the ignorance of the inhabitants will one day become proverbial.

It was probably from a conviction of this kind, that a few individuals of the town were induced to set on foot a public library, in hopes that, by rendering the knowledge to be derived from books of science and literature less expensive, many young persons, who generally spent their leisure hours to no rational purpose, might be attracted to the study of some of the best authors, and, by perseverance, make themselves not only more useful members of society, but also reflect honor on the place of their nativity.

This establishment, called the *Reading Permanent Library*, is raised on a small foundation, but such as has hitherto proved successful in most of the great towns in England; neither would the original intent of the institution admit of a larger subscription, without destroying the principal benefit that was expected to be derived from it, that of inducing the younger and lower classes to become members: accordingly it was agreed, that each member, on subscribing his name, should pay one guinea advance, and five shillings quarterly; the books never to be sold (except duplicates) and to be the joint property of the members, transferable at their option.------This society has been established two years, and during this period, they have purchased nearly 300 volumes, of the best modern authors, besides reviews, magazines, &c. and I am informed, that the shares are now worth three if not four pounds each.

But as every thing in this world must have its *fellow*; no sooner was this society established, with the most promising prospect of success, than pride, jealousy, or envy, attempted to stifle it in its cradle, by the establishment of another, on a more *magnificent* scale, worthy to be sure of this *incomparable borough, the pride and boast* of England, and *one of the principle gems* in the imperial crown. Accordingly a subscription was set on foot, for the purpose of raising 3000 pounds in twenty-five pound shares; but soon despairing of raising the intended sum by this means, the shares were raised to 30 pounds, compulsory on those who had at first subscribed only for the original sum: by this means, they were, at the commencement of last year enabled to form a society, called the Reading Literary Institution, though it has no one trait of an institute in it; being merely a library, with a reading-room for daily papers: the only thing wherein the other society is

inferior to it, if the want of that may be considered an inferiority, which may be supplied in every coffee-room and pot-house in the town. Each subscriber of 30 pounds is entitled to a share in the books; there are also nominal, or yearly subscribers, of two guineas each: these are intitled to read the newspapers, and such books as they may wish to see out of the library, but have no share in the stock. With this sum of 3000l. they took, as I am informed, a house at *forty pounds a year*, exclusive of taxes, which they fitted up in a good style, and placed in it a librarian at the rate of *one hundred pounds* per annum, he finding fire and candle: so that you see here is the interest of the whole three thousand pounds exhausted, supposing it had been all funded; but as it was necessary, that this society, so *honorable to the town*, should commence with *éclat*, the greater part of the money was expended in the purchase of books, and 3000l. 3 per cent. consols only were purchased: the interest arising from this sum will scarcely be sufficient to pay for periodical works and daily papers, without leaving any thing for the purchase of books: however they flatter themselves that the annual subscriptions will at least pay the expences of the house; and, as to books, they have already *more* than will ever *be read*, and therefore need no addition. From this state of their finances, you will suppose that the society must very soon die a natural death; but this is not very likely to happen, as the promoters of the scheme have introduced a clause into their agreement, that if the present price of shares should not be found adequate for the purpose, the subscription should be raised to the amount required.

If we make a comparison between the two societies, we shall find, the one, instituted for the good of the public at large; the other, for the benefit of a few individuals: the one, for accommodating those with high priced books of science, and general knowledge, whose humble situations in life would otherwise have deprived them the use of; the other for a lounging place, and to enable the subscribers to read books, which, however extravagant in price, they ought, as they are well able, to provide at their own expence. Upon the whole, were I a tradesman of Reading, I should prefer the former, and not only subscribe to it myself, but recommend my family, my apprentices, and servants to do the same. That nothing might be omitted to recommend this institution to public notice, the plan was ushered in by an *elegant* little poem, written by one of its founders; though short, it contained a variety of *beauties* very *uncommon* among the writers of the present day. To make an analysis of a poem like this, and at the same time to do *justice* to all its *merits*, would take more time than I can at present bestow upon it; besides the *genus irritabile vatum*, you know, tho' fond of *tickling*, are very apt to *wince* on being *scratched*. I shall therefore, content myself with recommending it to your perusal, not doubting but you will be as much struck with the variety of *beautiful passages* contained in it as I have been.

genus irritabile vatum: 'the irritable tribe of poets' (Horace).

The book most read here, is, as it doubtless ought to be, the Bible; next to that is *Moore's Almanack;* this may be found not only in every house in the town, but also in every one in the neighbourhood, and partakes nearly of the same degree of belief in its prognostications, as the Bible itself: strange as it may appear, that in the nineteenth century there should be found people, who can give credit to such impostors, or believe that men, by looking at the stars, can foretell the state

Moore's Almanack: this is still published, and probably doing quite well in this new age of mumbo-jumbo.

of the weather throughout the year, when even the wisest of themselves, cannot foresee what will follow in the space of the next 24 hours. But here their credulity does not stop: even whitchcraft, which is exploded in every other enlightened town in the kingdom, is as firmly believed here by many creditable people as the gospel. So late as the present century, a poor girl, the daughter of a tradesman, being convulsed in an extraordinary manner by fits, it was given out, that she was bewitched, and many well-meaning people among the sectaries, attended her, and even one of their ministers supported the delusion, by frequently praying by her bed-side, that she might be released from the machinations of the witch. The rumor of this extraordinary affair soon circulated through the town, and the house was crowded with visitors, to witness what they really believed to be the effect of some supernatural gift. Convinced in their own minds, that the girl was bewitched, it was no difficult matter to find out the witch, in the person of a respectable old woman, whose family it seems, had, for years, been suspected of possessing some extraordinary power of this sort; and as she was old, and possessed more understanding than the generality of people in her class in life, no doubt remained on the minds of these infatuated people, but that she was the secret agent of the poor girl's sufferings; and so persuaded were they of the fact, that it is impossible to say what might have been the consequences, had not *Lucina* stepped in at the end of *nine months,* and put an end to the charm, by relieving her at the same time from her burthen, and the supposed effects of witchcraft, to the no small confusion of the credulous multitude.-----Another of the same family, who gained a meritorious livelihood by retailing fruit, had always been suspected of being a witch, and what seemed

"confirmation strong as holy writ,"

it had been remarked by all the hucksters in the fruit market, that whenever they refused to take her offer for their goods,

she was bewitched: I have found no reference to this case in the *Mercury*; in 1773 it had reported that 'the ridiculous notion of witches and witchcraft still prevails among the lower sorts of people'.

Lucina: the Roman goddess of childbirth.

they were sure not to *sell them* that day. Such is the ignorance of the lower classes of people here! Whether they will ever be more enlightened, time will shew; but if they should, it will not be by attending methodist sermons, and pinning their faith on other men's sleeves, as ignorant as themselves; but by trying the strength of their own minds, and searching for truth in whatever quarter it may be found.-----Notwithstanding however this propensity for the marvellous, I do not find that there are any ghosts at present in Reading, except that which for a century past has resided in St. Mary's church-yard, in the form of a *white rabbit*: this fact I was told by a respectable acquaintance here, who, to convince me of the truth of it, very kindly offered to shew me the *monument* into which it was always seen to run whenever it was disturbed. Had he offered to shew me the identical *white rabbit,* it had been more to the purpose; but this, it seems, is a favor not always granted, for though it often shews itself to women and children, it is, like other ghosts, very *shy* of appearing before the incredulous.

As to works of science, history, or general information, few trouble themselves about them; and, as to religious books, they consult none but what are written by their own sect, or in support of their own religious opinions. A very good way, no doubt, to *come at the truth!*

Having given you the above imperfect sketch of the literary men this town has produced, and of the low state into which all degrees of literature have, for the two last centuries, been reduced here, I cannot conclude, without stating the pleasing hope I feel, that a few individuals, of the present day, are destined, by their present and future labors, not only to remove this opprobrium, but to give a lustre to their native place, equal to that of any other town in these kingdoms. As a proof of this statement, I need only mention Mrs. Le N--r, a lady possessed of great literary talent, evinced by her several publications, both in prose and verse, but the former are most admired, particularly her Village Anecdotes and Clara de Montfier. To make an analysis of the beautiful passages dispersed thro' these works would be only repeating what has been better said in all the Reviews and monthly publications; but what I conceive to be their greatest merit is, their general tendency to improve the morals of the reader, at the same time they afford him an abundant field of amusement.

I must also mention Miss M. R. M-----d, a young lady of great poetical talents, whose purity of sentiment, and elegance of diction, are equal to those of our best poets, while she excells most of them in the chastity of her style, and the harmony of her verse. A tender sensibility, the dictates of a good and feeling heart, pervades most of her pieces I have hitherto seen, which are generally of a serious cast. Should she ever publish a collection of her works, I am confident it would not only be a gratifying present to the public at large, but likewise do honor to this her native place.* To convince you that I am not guided by partiality in what I have said of this young lady, I have enclosed one of her poems for your perusal, which will, I think, convince you that the above is not an exaggerated account of her poetical merit.

Mrs. Le N--r: Elizabeth Le Noir, 1755–1841; daughter of the poet Christopher Smart; married a chevalier refugee; her *Village Anecdotes* of 1804 may have inspired Miss Mitford.

Miss M. R. M-----d: Mary Russell Mitford, then aged 22. She achieved considerable fame, not for verse but for sketches of rural and urban life in *Our Village*, aka Three Mile Cross, and *Belford Regis*, a thinly-disguised Reading. Her account of the town is polite, but a letter of 1813 reveals her true feelings: 'the Reading coach people, the Reading post people, and Reading altogether, was the most careless, blundering, unpunctual town ever heard of'.

native place: Miss Mitford was born in Alresford, Hants.

---

* The writer being a stranger, has, I fear, been misled in assigning Reading as the birth-place of this young lady; I believe, on enquiry, it will be found, that she is not a native, though she certainly came very young to this place. EDITOR.

To the Memory of Sir John Moore.

Who has not felt exulting rapture's glow,
For England's triumph o'er her haughty foe?
Who has not wept for for England's gallant train,
The slaughtered Victims of degenerate Spain?
Of every aid, of hope itself bereft,
Their firmness and their valor only left,
Let yon ensanguined plain their triumph tell;
Too dearly purchased – for their Leader fell!
In Victory's arms thus Abercrombie died;
Thus Nelson bled, our sorrow and our pride;
Still Britain mourns stern Fate's relentless doom,
And 'twines the Hero's laurels round his tomb.

Lamented Chieftain! Thy well-skilled command
From sure destruction saved thy faithful band;
'Twas thine with them each painful toil to share,
'Twas thine alone the mental pangs to bear,
When warring elements against thee rose,
Before thee treacherous friends—behind thee foes.
And when at length Corunna's towers appeared
And English vessels their proud ensigns reared,
'Twas thine to see thy bold Pursuers fly—
Nobly to conquer—undismayed to die.
Thy parting words to filial duty given;
And thy last thought to England and to Heaven.

No tawdry 'scutcheons hang around thy tomb;
No venal Mourners wave the sable plume:

No statues rise to mark the sacred spot;
No pealing organ swells the solemn note.

A hurried grave thy Soldiers' hands prepare;
Thy Soldiers' hands the mournful burthen bear;
The vaulted Sky to Earth's extremest verge
Thy Canopy: the Cannons' Roar thy dirge.

Affection's sorrows dew thy lowly bier,
And weeping Valor sanctifies the tear.

From the Rev. Mr. T.E.W————s, a gentleman of great learning, indefatigable industry, and superior abilities, much may be expected; and the specimens in botany, and other sciences, he has already given, as an author, are sufficient to prove his ability to treat with elegance and correctness, any subject he may choose to employ his pen upon.

To another branch of the same family, we are indebted for one of the best artists, as a landscape painter, this country ever produced. You know I am not a connoisseur in paintings, and therefore cannot be supposed to give this as my own private opinion, but as that of the great body of artists, whose unanimous approbation of his works, is a sufficient confirmation of their excellence.

The city of London is also under obligations to this town for one of its first architects, in the person of Mr. S---e; whose numerous works, in the city, and other parts of the kingdom, are convincing proofs of his superior abilities, in a line which has to boast of very few masters.

To this short but gratifying list of the natives of the town, who at present excell in different departments of the arts,

Rev. Mr. T.E.W————s: son of the T E Williams mentioned in Letter 7; he was chaplain of the gaol in 1811 and ran a school in Broad Street in 1819.

Mr. S---e: Despite his earlier strictures on the 'lamp post' in the Market Place, Man here recognises the genius of Sir John Soane, born (maybe) at Goring in 1753 and educated by William Baker at the very school which Man later took over. By 1810 he was well on with his greatest work, the Bank of England (largely destroyed in the 1920s and 30s); in 1789 he had built Simonds' new Reading brewery and brewer's house (totally destroyed in 1900). We use the words 'Georgian' and 'Victorian' to describe periods or styles, but it has been argued that the most significant architectural event of 1837 was not the Queen's accession but the death of Soane.

Capt. P----h: Lieutenant Parish, as he then was, played a part in the capture of Curacao in 1807. He was in the news again in 1809, capturing two Dutch vessels in the blockade of Holland, and 1813, when he took an American brig laden with sugar, coffee and indigo.

maybe added Capt. P----h, one of those heroes, who so nobly entered the harbour of Curaçoa, and stormed the batteries, in the face of a superior enemy; and who, on every occasion, has evinced an ardent desire to vindicate the glory and honor of his country.

I am, &c.
Reading, ------------

LETTER 5
on religion

To ------------

From the little value that has been hitherto set on literary attainments in this town, is, in a great measure, to be imputed that extravagance in religious creeds, which has, for nearly three centuries, prevailed here. No sooner was the reformation completed, than religious enthusiasm began to disturb the peace of families, and to threaten the destruction of the state. Here, as well as in other parts of the kingdom, the seeds of dissention were soon sown, and the harvest was such as might have been expected: the king was dethroned, and the constitution of the country was destroyed, to make way for an usurper, whose greatest recommendation and support was derived from sectaries, who agreed in nothing but their abhorrence of the established religion. At this period, fanaticism seems to have arrived at its highest pitch in this town, if we may judge from the following passage, in an assize sermon, preached in 1653, by the Rev. Simon Ford, vicar of St. Lawrence's:

"In this little town of Reading, I am verily persuaded, if *Augustine's and Epiphanius' catalogue of heresies* were lost, and all other modern and ancient records of that kind, yet it would be no hard matter to restore them with *considerable enlargements* from *this place*. They love

Anabaptism: there was an Anabaptist chapel near Man's house in 1802.

blasphemer: John Pordage 1607–81; Curate at St Laurence from 1644, Vicar of Bradfield 1647; branded a Bohemist, Familiarist and Leveller. One day in 1650 he abandoned a sermon, went into a trance and started dancing. His antics brought him before the Commissioners for Berkshire for Ejecting Scandalous and Insufficient Ministers.

Universalists: they held that all mankind will eventually be saved.

Sandemonians: correctly Sandemanians, they were a breakaway sect from the Glassites; both named for their founders.

Anabaptism, Familism, Socinianism, Pelagianism, Ranting, and what not; and that the *Devil was served* in *heterodox assemblies* as frequently as God in their's; and that one of the most eminent church livings in the county* was possessed by a blasphemer†; one, in whose house he believed, as some then present could testify, that the *Devil* was as *visibly familiar* as any *one of the family*."

Tho' this description of the sectaries of the preacher's days does not entirely coincide with those of the present time, the latter do not fall short of their ancestors, either in the variety or extravagance of their opinions. Among those of the present day, may be numbered the *Methodists, Calvinists, Baptists, Universalists, Quakers, Sandemonians,* and a verity of scions, under various denominations, springing out of that seminary of fanaticism----Methodism. Under pretence of a superior sanctity, and a greater correspondence to the doctrines of the Church, as set forth in the thirty-nine articles, homilies, and liturgy, these reformers have withdrawn from the established Church, (except where any of their preachers can intrude themselves) and erected in this place what they call a chapel, where they meet, and where service is performed, on certain days, almost incessantly, and where the unwary are at first drawn in by curiosity, and afterwards retained, not by conviction, but terror. The rant of their preachers, and the authoritative manner in which they portray the anger of the Almighty against unbelievers, (that is, those who do not attend the tabernacle) and the congratulations conferred on the members

---

* Bradfield.

† John Pordage.

of the society, who are designated as the *chosen of the Lord*, are arguments generally too powerful for men who never possessed just notions of Christianity, and too alarming to their fears to permit them to form a correct estimate between truth and falshood: thus they soon become proselytes *without conviction*, and desert their parish teachers, *without reason!* ————This sect has so much prevailed, through the terrors they inspire into weak minds, that two thirds of the inhabitants have withdrawn from the established churches within the town; and the roads, on the Sunday mornings, are thronged with taxed carts from the neighbouring villages, in open violation of that sabbath, which, in other respects, they affect to keep with so much sanctity; carrying a throng of ignorant infatuated farmers, and their families, who have been persuaded by terror to forsake the more enlightened preachers of their several parishes, to hear, what they are pleased to call *gospel* preaching, from some ignorant mechanic, who can scarcely write his own name. To such a length is the pretended sanctity of the sabbath-day carried, by these modern Sabbattarians, that some of the most bigoted among them will not suffer any work to be done in the family on that day; the dinner for Sunday must be dressed the day before, the cloth laid, and everything prepared the over-night, that nothing may prevent their attendance on the religious service of the Lord's day, as they affect to call Sunday. Not contented however with the observance of this principle among themselves, they have lately attempted to enforce it on those, who, still adhering to the established Church, presume to think, that the sanctity of that day will admit of a great deviation from the Jewish sabbath, which though commanded by the Almighty as *their lawgiver*, does not appear, from the tenor of the New Testament, to be binding on the followers of Christ: indeed they do not pretend to bring any proofs from Scripture in support of their system, but content themselves with quoting obsolete acts of parliaments, and holding out threats of persecution to those, who may be found infringing these statutes, by buying or selling on the Sunday; as if levying penalties on the guilty was *the best means of convincing them of their errors!* A Society for the Suppression of Vice was accordingly established, and a committee appointed to watch the tradesmen's doors on the Sunday morning, to lay informations before the magistrates, of such as presumed to sell any articles, however necessary to the subsistence of the buyers. In consequence of this system of *espionnage*, so abhorrent to the feelings of Englishmen, informations were soon laid before the magistrates, and the offending parties fined in the several penalties laid in these acts; but I have not heard that any have yet been levied. Indeed it was not to be expected, that the enlightened and humane magistrates, who preside over the police of this town, could lend their support to such a system of persecution; a persecution you will doubtless think an anomaly in the history of the Church, as being set on foot by a *tolerated sect* against the *members of the establishment.* As the magistrates did not seem inclined to sanction this species of persecution, a report was circulated that they would be compelled to do their duty, but the committee thought fit to deny this, in a letter addressed to a gentleman whom they had applied to, to solicit the charges they should have to bring before the magistrates, but whose integrity would not permit him to accept of their offer. In this letter, they say, "How far a magistrate might neglect or refuse to fulfil *his duty*, without its being proper to *oblige him to answer in a superior court of judicature*, is a question which the Reading Society *hopes they shall not have occasion to discuss!*" Evidently implying, that if in *their judgment* they should think the magistrate remiss in *his duty*, it would be their duty to remind him of it by a civil process.*

---

* See an excellent dissertation on this subject
  in the xxvi number of the Edinburgh Review.

This reply is in the true jesuitical style. Soon after the assassinations of Henry III. and IV. of France, one Santarelli, a Jesuit, published a book, wherein he asserted the Pope's right, not only of excommunicating, but also of dethroning Kings. The Parisians, who had so lately experienced the consequences of such doctrines, took the alarm, and the parliament not only ordered the book to be burned by the common hangman, but summoned Coton the provincial of the society to appear before them. Being asked, if he believed the Pope could excommunicate and depose the King of France — "*Ah!* (said he,) *the King is the eldest son of the Church, he will do nothing that shall compel the Pope to come to that extremity!*"* Compare this with the passage above quoted, and then judge.

Among the members of this society, there are undoubtedly many respectable characters, whose intentions are good, though their persuasion is erroneous; but there are many likewise, who conform to their extravagant notions on the *divine grace* and the *new birth*, not from principle or conviction, but from self interest, expecting to derive from their conformity, advantages in trade they could not otherwise obtain; there are others also, who, having passed their youthful days in debaucheries and profligacy, are glad to find shelter in a

---

* Il etait toujours question de cet horrible systeme de la puisance du Pape sur les Rois. Santarelli, jesuite Italien, publia cette doctrine, dans un nouveau livre par Vitelleski, general de cet ordre, et dedié au Cardinal de Savoie. Il fut brulé selon l'ùsage. Le parlement ordonne au provincial, de comparoitre le lendemain. Le jesuite Coton, alors provincial, porte le parole. On lui demande, s'il croit que le Pape puisse excommunier et deposser le Roi de France? Ah! répondit il, le Roi est fils aisné de l'eglise, il ne fera jamais rien qui oblige le Pape *à en venir à cette extrémité!*

Œuvres de Voltaire, tom. 20.

religious society, which affords a prospect of impunity in a future state, provided they have *faith*, which they pretend is a sufficient atonement for the past, without the performance of moral duties, or the other criterions of a Christian spirit, for the time to come. That this should be the case, cannot be surprising to any one, who observes the eagerness they express to receive into their body every one that offers to join them, for the purpose of swelling their annual returns; contrary to the conduct of another religious sect, who always put out of their communion every one that evinces any irregularity in their moral duties, or a deviation from their established principles. To the Methodists may be applied, with more propriety, what has been said of the Calvinists, "that they profess *a religion without morality*, and *worship a God without mercy*."

Among the other contrivances to promote the spreading of this society, that of private meetings at the houses of some of its members, has been adopted with peculiar success. They well knew, that many respectable inhabitants were unwilling to be seen at their places of public worship; this prejudice could only be overcome by institutions less public, and this of private meetings appeared to be the most ready means of overcoming this obstruction to their ultimate success. It was impossible that in a community like this, but an intimate connection must subsist between some of its members and many respectable characters, who had not sanctioned their schism by their presence; these therefore were to be got over, and no method could be better devised for the purpose, than to tempt them to attend the evening lectures at Mr. ——'s, where, if they were once entered, they knew their *conviction* would soon follow, and the step from the conventicle to the meeting-house would be a matter of course. Thus many well-meaning persons in the higher ranks are, by degrees, induced to join them, as well as many of the poorer classes, who are easily *converted,* as it is called, by the hopes of partaking of the charities founded at these places, for such as attend their meetings.

The success which these modern enthusiasts have had, in perverting the minds of the ignorant classes of society, has been generally imputed to the negligence of the established clergy, in the performance of their ecclesiastical functions; but I can by no means agree to this opinion, as the Church never possessed more learned, pious, and devout pastors, than she does in the present times, nor men who took more pains in the exercise of their ministry, or set better examples of holy living to their parishioners; so much so, that it is as difficult to point out one among their number, who has deviated from the strict path of duty he is expected to follow, as a minister of the gospel, as it is to find one among their opponents, whose conduct is wholly irreproachable; we must therefore seek for another cause, to account for the general mass of the lower classes forsaking their Parish Churches and the religion of their forefathers; and this, if I mistake not, will be found to have arisen from the facility offered to the lowest mechanic, by the existing laws, of obtaining, at the quarter sessions, at the small expence of six-pence, a licence to open a conventicle, and obtrude himself, and his crude opinions, into parishes where the Constitution has already provided a proper minister to perform the necessary religious offices. Novelty always raises a curiosity, which every one is eager to satisfy; thus stimulated, the parishioners flock to the new conventicle—the seeming earnestness of the preacher claims their attentions—his vehemence is mistaken for oratory—his rhapsodies, though not understood, are admired as sublime— and the familiar manner, in which he introduces the Deity, and his misconceptions of his attributes, are considered as a proof of great powers, because they come within the compass of their own confined ideas of the *personality* of the Almighty. Their rude, unlettered, teachers are all *Anthropomorphites!* The personification of the Deity is one of the most successful engines they employ in this great business of reformation from *light* to *darkness!* It is in conformity to the literal sense of the Scriptures, "*In the image of God created he him.*" It comes within the powers of our conceptions, and thus, being familiar to our ideas, requires no stretch of the understanding to enforce conviction on the mind: having thus, as it were, confined the Deity to locality, it is easy to introduce him, with all the *human* passions, and to portray him, as having *kindled his wrath* against the human race; that *his vengeance* is at hand against all unbelievers, (that is, those who are not members of *their* societies) and that all the children of Adam are destined to *eternal misery*, unless they are regenerated and become members of *their* church. With such facilities to obtain the liberty of preaching, and with such doctrines to terrify their hearers, can it be wondered, that so many converts are daily made?----As well might the miller complain that his water was withdrawn from his mill, while he suffered the banks to be *perforated* in every part; as for any one to be astonished at the increase of methodism, while such facilities for preaching are suffered to remain. Let the *out-lets* to the water be first stopped, and it will soon return to its usual channel.

Anthropomorphites!: they believed that God took a human form.

The next religious establishment in this place is, that of the Calvinists, under which denomination are united the Presbyterians and Independents; these were, 'till within these few years, distinct congregations, but the latter having declined in numbers, so as to have been incapable of maintaining an established preacher, the remainder joined the Presbyterians, with whom they now form one congregation. They are not so numerous as the Methodists, but more respectable in character. Composed mostly of ancient families, who have been educated in the tenets of their forefathers, to which they tenaciously conform: and under the guidance of a regular-bred clergyman, who is an honor to his profession, they are more steady in the belief of their own church, and less eager to disturb the peace of their neighbours, by the desire of making proselytes to their opinions, than those, who having lately adopted new systems of belief, are induced to propagate them, as a sanction for their own versatile conduct. They are, in general, pious without affectation, and religious without hypocrisy; correct in their manners, strict in their moral duties, and meritorious in every part of their conduct through life. Like the Methodists, however, with whom, by the way, I think they have more closely connected themselves, than can be justified by prudence, they are all proselytes to the prevailing opinion of the sanctity of the sabbath-day. In consequence of this connection, they constantly attend the popular preachers of this sect, join in their animosities against the established church, and further their views, by apparently swelling their numbers in their annual returns; while they, in return, cherish the intention of shaking them off whenever they shall, as they fondly hope, supersede the established Clergy.

The Baptists likewise are a numerous congregation, but chiefly composed, as they generally have been, from the lower classes of people. This sect, having no regular seminary for the education of their ministers, any one among them, however ill-qualified to perform the sacred duties, is admitted into the pulpit, if approved of by the flock. From this want of education however, their Sermons, or whatever they may be called, are peculiarly suited to the level of the meanest understandings; though incapable of attracting the attention of the higher orders, notwithstanding the fundamental article of their belief is much more consonant to the Scriptures, than the mode of sprinkling, adopted by other churches. Like the other sectaries, these people have a high opinion of the sanctity of the Sabbath, and conform to it with the strictest punctuality; indeed this notion is gaining ground daily, even in our own Church; so much so, that instead of *books of sports and pastimes*, as in the days of Charles I. we are assailed on all sides with exhortations on the supposed sanctity of the day; but I do not remember that any one has taken the pains to prove his opinion, either from the words or *practice* of our Saviour, or the writings of his Apostles.

We are all the children of opinion, and are easily led by high *sounding words*. You and I remember the time, when Good-Friday was considered as a day peculiarly set a-part for sports and pastimes, but of late years, one of our bishops having, at the end of nearly *eighteen centuries* after the crucifixion, discovered, for the *first time*, that it ought, on the contrary, to be kept as a day of fasting and prayer, the discovery was echoed in every quarter; the holiness of the day has since been annually recommended by the public functionaries, who must be allowed to be great proficients in the knowledge of scripture, and without further investigation adopted by the nation at large. In like manner, the first day of the week was at first set a-part for a fixed time of prayer, but unconnected with the restraints of the Jewish Sabbath, and as long as the Catholic religion presided over this nation, the people were contented to call it Sunday; soon after the reformation, it began to be the fashion among the dissenters to distinguish it as the Sabbath, and as such more particularly dedicated to prayers and

long sermons; since that, the modern sectaries have gone a step further, calling it the *Lord's day*, and under the sanction of this name, prohibit their followers from the enjoyment of the Sabbath as a day of rest and relaxation from the labors of the week. It is a day however, for which I am more grateful to the Jewish legislator than for any other of his regulations, because this alone, in the whole week, affords a poor man a clean shirt, a hot dinner, and the comfortable enjoyment of his family. Let him not therefore be deprived of the liberty of enjoying it innocently, in whatever way he pleases, nor compel him to pass that day in moody melancholy, which was intended by his Maker for his happiness. For my own part, I am convinced, that the Almighty views with more complacency an assembly of French peasants dancing, on a Sunday evening, to the sound of a cracked violin, than in the superabundant zeal of our English enthusiasts, singing hymns, or listening to the rant of an ignorant preacher, on a summer's evening, in a confined room, where they are nearly par-boiled by the steam of their own breaths, and from whence an effluvia issues, that, in a literal sense, tends to *poison* the whole neighbourhood.

The Quakers here, as in most other places, are a very respectable body of people; they are not numerous, but in every respect support the character they have justly obtained for their industry, sobriety, and a scrupulous observance of the moral duties; virtues more advantageous to society, than the boasted refinements of modern reformers, who confine their actions to speculative opinions of virtue, that must ultimately end in a dereliction of every thing that has hitherto been considered as the criterion of a true Christian. That this sect is not numerous, must be accounted for from the care they take

Quakers: Man is kinder to them than Cobbett. George Fox visited Reading in 1655.

of excluding from their society all such as deviate from the dictates of sound morality: this is certainly commendable; and had they confined themselves to the exclusion of such only, no one could have censured their conduct; but when I see them, as in a late instance, excluding from their church men of the most enlightened minds, strict in their moral duties, and whose conduct through life would do honor to any church, merely for speculative opinions respecting the payment of tythes, and other matters of little consequence; I cannot help regretting, that such a spirit of persecution should have found its way among the members of a society, in other respects, so deserving the approbation of every good man.

There are a great many *Jews* here, but so *poor*, they can never afford to give any thing in charity, however distressing the case, or worthy the object. This, perhaps, may be the reason, that they have no established *Synagogue*, or place of worship, as the expence would be too great; however they at all times pay a proper *devotion* to the *counter*; and their *shop-books* are not unfrequently kept by *double entry*. Political affairs they do not trouble themselves much about, except so far as they influence the price of stocks; on these they dream night and day; and if you happen to fall into the company of one of these modern *Israelites*, all his conversation turns on the new loan, or the rise or fall of the market. I often wonder at the folly of my contemporaries of this description, whose solitary ideas are absorbed in accumulating wealth, which in a few hours they may be called upon to leave, to some relative, who will laugh in his sleeve at the folly of his benefactor denying himself necessaries of life, for no other purpose than to have it said at his death, *What a great fortune he left behind him!* Or,

no established *Synagogue*: Reading's Jews met in a house in Body Road from 1888; the Goldsmid Road synagogue opened in 1900.

***double entry*:** In Man's conventionally anti-Jewish passage, 'double entry' sounds like a pejorative term, suggesting false accounting; but all uses in the *OED* are straightforward.

to use a favorite expression here, *How well he cut up!* or, *Could he have taken it with him to bribe Minos or Rhadamanthus!* Perhaps there had been some sense in it, but to be continually heaping up, without enjoying the fruits of our riches, during the short time it could be of any use to us, is surely one of the grossest follies a reasonable being can fall into.

The French emigrants have a Catholic chapel here, frequented by some few families of that persuasion, who have long been inhabitants of the town. So far is right: I would have every one enjoy his own religious creed without molestation; but let him stop there. While he enjoys his own belief, he ought not to disturb that of others, by being continually on the watch to make converts, as is too much the case with all sects, except the Church of England, who, contented with the power she possesses, leaves every one to be governed by his own conscience.

Perhaps none of the mistaken duties of religion have done more harm to society, than the desire of proselytism, so common to all sects: 'tis this spirit that now threatens the overthrow of the British power in India, where missionaries are sent at a great expence, Bibles distributed, (to which the society here has contributed largely) and every means taken to introduce a new religion, not called for by the people, nor sanctioned by the Deity, who would not have suffered so many of his creatures to continue so long in error, if such it be, without taking some means of enlightening their minds, or *expressly* commissioning some other people to convert them. This he has no where done, tho' every one takes upon himself the office, as if by his authority. True it is, he has said "*Go ye, and teach all nations*;" &c. But to whom did he give

Minos or Rhadamanthus!: sons of Zeus and Europa who became judges – and therefore bribable – in the underworld.

French emigrants: These were priests who fled the Revolution after 1789; some were billetted in the King's Arms on Castle Hill. The first post-reformation RC church in Reading was the Chapel of the Resurrection, set up in 1812 on the site of the present Rising Sun pub opposite Apex Plaza.

this command? To the Apostles at Jerusalem; *not* to barbers, tinkers, and tailors turned preachers, of a country not known at the time but as a horde of barbarians! Was it likely that Jesus should have commissioned people born almost *two thousand* years after his time, to go more than *ten thousand* miles, to convert a people, whom, if it had been his pleasure, he could so easily have done long ago? My good, honest, well-meaning countrymen, recollect that the Apostles, tho' so much nearer India, did not think themselves bound by a *general* order to attempt the conversion of these people; and why, therefore, should you, who are so far off, and in good truth have received no order whatever? But suppose you should even succeed in the attempt; what benefit would arise to the inoffensive, harmless natives, by their becoming Christians? Would they be better men? No! More honest, or more humane? No! What then must be the consequence of this proselyting system, but to introduce *discord* where harmony exists? and to disturb the peace of families? as is experienced here about *justification by faith,—the new birth,—putting off the man of sin*, and a hundred more absurdities of the like sort, which you will never be able to explain to them intelligibly, because in reality *unintelligible*: they are equally unintelligible to yourselves, and have only been introduced by your preachers, as an *easy* succedaneum for morality, which you affect to despise, because it is difficult to *practice*.

By making the natives of India, whether Mahomedans or Pagans, Christians, unless you enlighten their minds and purify their hearts, all the *good* that will be derived from their conversion will be, that the *Mussulmans* will learn to eat pork; and the disciples of *Vishnou*, for the gratification of their appetites, will be taught to eat every description of flesh; and to take away the lives of those very *animals* they now cherish with so much care and anxiety. But you will say, perhaps, that by becoming Christians, they will ensure their future happiness in a world to come. It may be so; but unless you make them better men than you can yourselves boast of being, I think you might as well forbear intruding where you have no business, and leave all mankind *to stand or fall to their own master.*

I have been led to these observations, because these *emigrès* I mentioned, not content with the indulgences they have met with here, are, I am told, endeavouring to make proselytes of the inhabitants, particularly women and children; some of the latter sing the *gloria patri* and *de profundis* admirably already; and the women are furnished with *Latin missals*, to their great edification, no doubt. This, I think, if true, should be put a stop to; not that I am afraid of their absurd tenets gaining much ground among us; for what Englishman could, in these enlightened times, and *particularly in Reading*, believe, that a priest could *make* his *God* and then *eat him?* or that it is his duty to pray to men like himself, under the name of saints, many of whom deserved hanging instead of an apotheosis, and who, if they were what in reality they are pretended to have been, could not be present every where, like the Deity, to hear their prayers? It is not therefore through any apprehension of their success, that I think this disposition should be curbed; but because I am persuaded, that as far as it tends to create divisions in private families, it is of a dangerous tendency. Let there be *a variety of sects* in the world; well and good, but *one* only must be the *lot* of each family, to ensure domestic happiness.

Amidst the chaos of religious opinions, and superstitions, I am happy to say, that there are very few Deists here: whether the soil is not *congenial* to their growth, or whether, like those in other places, they take no pains to disseminate their principles, certain it is, there are not a dozen families of this description in the whole town. That men should be so blind to their future happiness, as to renounce the hope of their salvation, because their *feeble reason* cannot comprehend the hidden and revealed mysteries of the gospel, is such a perversion of the understanding, as is hardly creditable, had we not daily instances of this sad melancholy *truth!* May we, my friend, take warning from their lost state; and while we pray for their conversion; let us, like all good men, embrace with faith whatever is recorded in the Holy Scriptures, however inconsistent with our ideas; and believe, with the Church, that none can be saved, but through the merits of the Lord Jesus Christ, though we may not understand, why an *imputed* righteousness should have more weight in the sight of God, in the day of judgment, than a life spent in the performance of every virtue under Heaven, but without faith!

There are a few persons here, who *keep a seraglio*; but as these generally unite the love of *women with wine*, I think they cannot properly be called *Mahomedans*; else they would have afforded me an opportunity of finishing this account of the religious sects here with a very *proper climax*. As it is, I have no doubt, you will admire the variety of our refinements in religious opinions, and with a late French writer, be astonished, that the same country should have produced a *Locke* and a *Newton*, a *Methodist* and a *Moravian!*

Besides the above, there are several other religious societies here; but, as they are all founded on methodistical principles, they may be classed among their number, and included in the same description. I shall therefore not detain you longer, with a subject which, I fear, has already tired your patience; but, as I wished to give you a faithful picture of this place and its inhabitants, I could not refrain from treating fully a subject that forms so striking a feature in it.

I am, &c.
Reading, ––––––––––––

LETTER 6
on government and politics

To ------------

This town, like many others, owes its foundation to a religious house, founded here in the time of the Saxon Octarchy, which, though soon after destroyed, and the houses reduced to ashes by the Danes, revived in the subsequent reign of Henry I. in consequence of the magnificent Abbey founded here by that prince, in the 12th century, the ruins of which still remain.

Saxon Octarchy: not joint government by eight, but eight separate kingdoms. Considered to be a heptarchy until Sharon Turner's *The History of the Anglo-Saxons* (1805).

At first, the inhabitants formed themselves into a society called the Guild-merchant, and endeavored to exclude all others from trading in the town, but they were not sanctioned by a royal Charter 'till after the Conquest, for which reason this is called a Borough by prescription.

The first Charter granted to the Corporation was in the reign of Henry III. This, I believe, is not now in existence; but is referred to in that of Edward I. which, in consequence of a Latin term used in it, is called a Charter by *inspeximus*. These Charters were renewed by each of the succeeding monarchs, but conferred neither judicial nor civil powers on the Guild-merchant before the Reformation, being only Charters of Liberties as they are called, granting permission to the inhabitants to buy and sell all over the kingdom, to set up stalls at fairs, and an exemption from paying toll for passing bridges. During all which time the Abbot and Monks governed the town under their foundation Charter, granted by Henry I.

inspeximus: this merely meant that the king claimed to have read his predecessor's charter before renewing it.

93

with as ample powers, as it is therein expressed, as he himself possessed.

After this period, the Corporation began, by possessing themselves of the prerogatives of the Abbots, to assume nearly their present power and authorities, afterwards confirmed to them by the Charter of Charles I. This is the present governing Charter, though they subsequently received others from Oliver Cromwell, Charles and James II.

The present Corporation consists of thirteen Aldermen, one of which is alternately Mayor, except he is excused from absence, or for having served the office a stated number of times; and twelve Burgesses, who become Aldermen by seniority, as often as vacancies happen in their number, by decease or otherwise. These, by their Charter, are authorised to elect a High Steward, who is generally some nobleman connected with the town by his residence in the neighbourhood, a Steward or Recorder, a Town Clerk, Coroner, and three Serjeants at Mace.

At the quarter-session, the Mayor presides in the court, assisted by the Recorder, for the trial of misdemeanors, committed within the boundaries of the Corporation. He also holds a Court-leet every Wednesday, for the settlement of differences among the inhabitants, and other Corporation business. On his entering into office, he appoints his own Constables, and during his mayoralty can set the assize of bread, beer, and wine; but this privilege has not been asserted for nearly a century past, and, in consequence, the dealers in these articles have, during that time, affixed their own prices to their wares, with the exception of the bakers, who in general regulate the price of bread according to the assize in London, allowing a small diminution for the difference of the carriage of the flour downwards to that port. On going out of office, the Mayor is a Justice of the Peace for the Borough, for the year ensuing, and is not liable to serve again, according to the present mode of election, 'till it becomes his turn in rotation, though formerly the office was elective, and many instances occur of the same person serving it several years successively. The senior Alderman is styled the Father of the Corporation,

The present Corporation: until 1833 this body was a self-selecting, self-perpetuating, conservative oligarchy.

and as such is excused from serving the office of Mayor in future: this is no small privilege, as the duties are sometimes very difficult and trying, and the expence considerable. It has been customary here, as in other Boroughs, on his entering into office, for the Mayor to invite the principal inhabitants of the town and some of the gentlemen in the neighbourhood to an elegant dinner at the Town-hall. For this, I am informed, he is only allowed 20 pounds from the Corporation-fund, though it seldom costs less than 200, besides other expences, which must be incurred within the year; and the only emoluments he receives, in return, are a few fee-farm rents, generally paid in fowls at Michaelmas and Christmas, agreeable to a covenant inserted in all the Corporation leases. This is the general practice, and I believe is never omitted.

It has long been a subject of debate, whether Corporations are a benefit, or a nuisance to society? For my own part, judging from the observations I have been able to make in the little time I have been in this borough, I have no hesitation in giving my opinion, that they are in their nature and practice calculated to be of great service to the community, and particularly so in this town, where I am told justice is always administered by them without partiality, or respect of persons, the poor as well as the rich being equally protected in their persons and properties; indeed where all the parties are known to each other, the judge, the jurors, and the prisoner, it is impossible that unjust prejudices can prevail, to the injury of any one, without being soon detected. The expedition with which civil and criminal disputes are settled here on the spot, without waiting for the assizes or county sessions, oftentimes held at a great distance, is another

advantage derived to the inhabitants of this Corporation; as is likewise the exemptions from serving on juries in any other than the town courts, and from the payments towards the county rates. This Borough being a county within itself, is only bound to maintain its own police, and this is done at the expence of the Corporation alone: it is at their expence the prisons and places of confinement are provided and kept in repair, and the prisoners maintained. The officers of the police are their servants, and paid by them; they also repair and keep clean a considerable proportion of the pavements, particularly in the Market-place; and the bridges, which are here numerous, are kept in constant repair by them, and an elegant stone bridge, of one eliptic arch and stone balustrades, has been erected by them within these few years; in addition to this, the Town-hall has been rebuilt and enlarged, and all the alms-houses placed on the most respectable footing, without costing the inhabitants one penny. This being the case here, as it really is, you cannot be surprised, if I confess myself a friend to the Corporation system. There are faults in it, no doubt, which might be amended, and particularly as under the present system, the members being a self-elected body, have it in their power to confine their civic honors to their own relatives or party friends, and, by a kind of *family compact*, monopolize to themselves the jurisdiction of the town through many generations. Had the elective franchise been adopted in the choice of the Corporate body, many of the abuses and peculations of the former magistrates, so justly complained of by the inhabitants, might have been prevented; but this was not in Archbishop Laud's contemplation, when he obtained the governing Charter of Charles I. for the town.

a county: Reading was a County Borough until 1974.

That prelate being, perhaps, justly inimical to a system that caused so much trouble to himself and his royal master, took care, in wording the Charter, to keep the elective principle entirely out of sight, by drawing up the different articles so as to form the Corporation into a separate and distinct body, entirely independent of the people they were to govern, and by leaving to their discretion alone the filling up all vacancies that might happen, either by death or resignation.* Notwithstanding, however, this, and a few other defects in the original construction of this Corporation, I am still inclined to think, that more benefits are derived from it than the inhabitants are generally inclined to admit.

This Borough has regularly sent Members to Parliament ever since the commencement of the reign of Edward I. but in what manner they were elected, or who were the electors, is uncertain, whether the Corporation or the inhabitants, but it most probably was the former, as the people, at that early period, were considered very little superior to slaves, if they were not really such, who were entitled to none of

---

* The following extract from the introduction to the Charter, written probably by Laud himself, is, perhaps, the most possitive assertion of the divine right of Kings, ever penned by an Englishman:

"Whereas in every Monarchy, the *health of the People doth depend upon the Crown, and all authority is derived from the Prince, and Kings are for that purpose authorized in the sublime seat of Majesty,* that as Fathers of the Country they should protect the People *committed to them by the King of Kings,* that with the *dew of their benignity, they should refresh* their faithful subjects, either employed in trading, or any other way whatever, concerning the good of the Commonwealth, and that they should substitute subordinate Officers, who for the administration of justice, and the conservation of the Peace, should be Rulers over Cities and other places of their territories, and over the People inhabiting the same, &c." EDITOR

the privileges belonging to free-men, nor had any right to participate in the government of the country. If the Corporate body were the electors, it was natural that they should call upon the Master of the Guild, or one of its members, to represent the Borough, as the most proper person, to guard the rights and privileges of the free-men; and accordingly in looking over the list of Members, given in Mr. Coates' History of this place, I find this to have been the case for nearly three centuries; during all which period, I believe none but inhabitants of the town were ever chosen to fulfil the important duties of this office. Under this system, when few could be found willing to accept of a trust replete with difficulties and dangers to whoever was delegated to support the rights of the people in opposition to an arbitrary government, it became customary, and even necessary, to allow each Member 2s. a day for his charges, while attending the Parliament. This expence, as the sessions were very short, seldom exceeded five pounds in a year, but small as this sum was, it was found so oppressive to many Corporate towns that they petitioned Parliament to be relieved from the burthen incurred by their sending Members to represent them; and tho' this borough did not go quite so far, yet they frequently found it very difficult to raise the necessary sum for the purpose, and on one occasion did not scruple to evade it, not in the most honorable way.

At what time the present mode of electing gentlemen from any part of the kingdom began, I am not certain, but it was probably about the period of the civil war, which so convulsed the country as to overturn most of the former usages, by introducing new ones better adapted to the times. However this may be, although as in a late instance a preference has sometimes been given to a Town's-man, the representation of the borough has, for a long time, been open to any gentleman, however distant his residence, who may be desirous of obtaining a seat in Parliament.

There can be no doubt but the mode of election here has frequently varied, especially in the persons entitled to give their votes; whether they were originally the Corporation only, as I said before, is uncertain, but if they were, a great innovation was made in the reign of Charles II. as, about that period, I find, the inhabitants at large, under the appellation of *Pot-wablers*, returning the Members. To claim this right, it was necessary, if the person was not an established householder, to make himself conspicuous to his neighbours, by the act of boiling a pot in the open streets, on the day previous to the election, which gave rise to the absurd appellation.

But the scenes of riot and confusion exhibited by the common people on these occasions, and the frequent contested returns brought before the House of Commons, occasioned the legislature, in the reign of Queen Ann, to declare the right of election in future, to be in the inhabitants paying scot and lot, with whom it still continues, but their number is much diminished, from the operation of the poor's laws. The elections being thus placed in such respectable hands, it is natural to suppose, that this must be one of the most virtuous and independent boroughs in the kingdom; and so it is, if you will take the good people's word for it, who are always boasting of their *patriotism*, their *independence*, their *public spirit*, and the *purity* of their *suffrages*, not without, at the same time, casting a few side-winded reflexions on a neighbouring borough or

Pot-wablers: originally 'potwaller', from Old English 'weallan', to boil; frequently corrupted to potwobbler or potwalloper.

two, where they insinuate every man has his price paid at a concerted time, by a person called the *miller*. Whether these assertions be true or false, is more than I know; but if Corruption has really quitted this place, it must have been of late

miller: millers had enjoyed a reputation for dishonesty since Chaucer's time; I have not found this specific use of the word in any dictionary.

years only, for at the bottom of the Poll-paper for the election in 1754 is the following *nota benè*: "Upwards of 50 persons who *voted* against Lord Fane *promised to vote for his Lordship*, near *forty of whom polled singly for Mr. Dodd.*" And in 1768, I find the following paragraph, in the Annual Register:——"At Abingdon assizes, *four verdicts were obtained for bribery* in the *late election for the Borough of Reading*, and it is said that *divers other prosecutions, upon the same statute, are depending in that Borough.*" It was at this election, that several of the poorer voters who had taken money, on finding it necessary to take the oath against bribery, before they were admitted to vote, actually brought the money they had received, as the wages of iniquity, and threw it down on the table in the hustings, in face of the very candidates by whose agents it had been given. And so far was this disgraceful system carried at this time, that some who had intruded themselves on the candidates, as agents to conduct their election, actually sent some of their old shop goods to the more indigent voters, as presents from the candidates, which they afterwards charged in their accounts, as the price of a purchased vote, when at the same time that vote had been given gratuitously, thus defrauding the man they pretended to serve, and blackening the characters of honest voters, without their being able, from the privacy of the act, to be sensible of the injury done them, and consequently to vindicate themselves, in the eyes of their deceived friends, from so wicked a calumny. Thus you see, that at no very distant date, the good people of this *immaculate* borough could condescend to receive a visit from the *miller* as well as their neighbours; and if he has not been seen *here* of late, it is only because their descendants have changed the *mode* not the *substance* of corruption, so as to make it somewhat more *palatable* to their stomachs, and more consonant to the refinements of the present age.

You will hardly believe me, perhaps, when I assure you, that notwithstanding all their display of integrity in the choice of their Representatives, a seat in Parliament, for this place, does not cost the successful candidate less than four thousand pounds, and this without any man actually receiving a farthing by way of a bribe. This, however, is easily conceived, if you consider the current expences on the day of election cannot be less than one thousand pounds, including a public dinner for all the electors, in addition to the one annually held here, which is the *sine quâ non* on these occasions; for without it a candidate would stand a very poor chance of success at a future election. But this you know cannot be called *bribery*, because altho' every one that partakes of it costs the Member *a guinea,* none of them carry it away in their *pockets.* The eagerness evinced by these public-spirited electors to pay themselves by eating and drinking, has been encouraged by one of their present Members, who gives an annual dinner to about four hundred persons, at the expence of nearly as many hundred pounds. To the money thus wasted in the encouragement of gluttony and inebriety, may be added subscriptions to every charitable fund; and even the Literary Institution, which I mentioned to you in a former letter, has *condescended* to accept his bounty of *two hundred and forty pounds*, notwithstanding most of the members of that society are men of large fortunes, and known to be inimical to his interest. This instance of meanness displayed by some of the first people here, is a convincing proof that a sordid disposi-

one of their present Members: Charles Shaw Lefevre: Miss Mitford says he was given to making tolerably bad puns. Reading had only 560 parliamentary electors in 1802, and local democracy was non-existent. But having two members for one constituency did provide a crude sort of proportional representation.

The other gentleman: John Simeon; his brother Edward was Governor of the Bank of England.

tion is not confined to the lower classes only, but has taken possession of those who ought to be patterns of purity to their inferiors.

The other gentleman, supported by his brother, has taken a different, and I think, in some instances, a better method of attaining the same end, by contributing to the relief of the necessitous, in various ways; to persons in trade, money is lent at 4 per cent. or they are assisted in the purchase of their raw materials, and in the disposal of their manufactures. The sons of some of the electors have been *quartered* on the Bank, and those of others have been provided for in the East and West Indies. Clothes are distributed among the poor; and their children are once a year regaled with plum-cake, in the Market-place, not you may be assured for a *vain display of a charitable act*, but as an incitement to others to do the same. They are members and supporters of all the benefit societies and clubs, and a Director of the Bank of England has been frequently seen decorated with a grotesque wig, a frightful mask, and the most ridiculous dress that can be conceived, presiding at a Club of ODD FELLOWS.

All these methods are dignified by their partizans with the appellation of *heaven-born charities,* while their opponents stigmatise them as political engines contrived to deceive those who are not aware of the snare. It is not for me to decide this knotty point.

Non nostrum: a misquote from Virgil: 'it is not for the likes of us to settle such great matters'.

"Non nostrum est has componere lites."

I shall therefore content myself with relating the following anecdote, and leave you to draw what conclusion you please from it:

A certain humane gentleman one day asked his fishmonger, if he ever boiled his crabs alive? O! no, Sir; never; *I* always *kills* them first. I am very glad to hear it, returned the gentleman, as nothing can be better proof of a *humane* disposition, which you must certainly possess in a high degree, than to take the speediest and least painful means of putting to death those animals that Providence has provided for our support. Yes, indeed, Sir, *I kills* them first, because I found, when they were boiled alive they always *kicked off their legs!**

Such are the means whereby the boasted independence of this borough is supported, or perhaps I ought rather to say undermined. Indeed it appears to me very paradoxical, whether the electors here have any just idea of the true meaning of the word *independence*; as they seem to think they are perfectly *independent* in the choice of their members, when in fact they have no other resource left on the day of election, (unless they would subject themselves to the imputation of *ingratitude*,) than to return those on whose bounty they had previously been fattening for five or six years. This truism is so well understood here, that it is confessed by each party, that a new candidate would stand a poor chance for success on the day of an election, in opposition to the present Members, however great his merit, his independence, or the purity of his conduct as a public character: add to this, that the Corporation, by the manner of letting their estates, can, I

---

* I must confess myself somewhat at a loss to discover the author's meaning here, unless he would insinuate that a certain gentleman's *humane* disposition towards his Brother Town's-men, like the fishmonger's towards the crabs, took its rise from self-interested motives, in the year 1802, when the Member might fairly be said to have *kicked his own legs off!* EDITOR

am told, always command nearly *one hundred* votes, and then say if this is a free borough? You are not however to suppose by what is here said, that there are none here of a truly independent spirit; far from it, there are many of that description, but their number is inadequate to prevent these unjustifiable means being resorted to, to pervert the integrity of the lower classes, and, by thus forestalling their votes, bringing that disgrace on the town in which they find themselves unjustly implicated.

Attempts have been made, but without success, to put a stop to the giving of *public dinners*, and to turn *Corruption* under the *disguise* of *Charity*, out of the borough. Should this much to be wished for reformation be ever accomplished, then, and not 'till then, can this be considered *a free, unbiassed, and independent borough.*

I am, &c.
Reading, ------------

LETTER 7
a tour of the district

To —————

—————-Now the soft hour
Of walking comes: for him who lonely loves
To seek the distant hills, and there converse
With Nature.

Thomson's Summer

This place is so admirably situated in the heart of one of the finest counties in England, watered by two noble rivers, and crossed by numerous gravel roads, kept in the best order, that it is impossible to judge of the beauty of the surrounding scenery without visiting in person every part of it. I have therefore been frequently tempted to make short excursions to the neighbouring places, and always returned highly gratified.

About two miles to the eastward of this place is the pleasant and extensive village of Sonning, affording a delightful walk by the verdant side of the Thames, which is here nearly as wide as at London-bridge. If you go by the turnpike-road the distance is something greater, but in your way you pass the seat of Sir William Scott, in front of which is a small park laid out with taste. The house is neat, and affords a bird's-eye view of the Oxfordshire hills ranging along in front of it.

At Sonning is that delightful spot called Home Park, originally belonging to the Rich's family, many of whose remains

nearly as wide as at London-bridge:
Man is wrong: with the help of the Loddon, Wye, Colne, Wey, Mole, Hogsmill, Crane, Brent and Wandle, the Thames swells to three times its width in 60 miles.

seat of Sir William Scott: Erlegh Court, demolished 1935.

Home Park: Holme Park.

Palmer: Richard Palmer, not related to the biscuit family, bought the estate in 1802.

present elegant mansion: The plain 1796 house was encased in flint and brick by Henry Woodyer in 1881; it is now occupied by the Blue Coat School.

are deposited in the parish church adjoining the park-wall. The late Admiral Sir Thomas Rich, bart. in whom the title expired, alienated the estate to ——— Palmer, esq. who took down the old dilapidated building, and erected the present elegant mansion in a more commanding situation. The house is situated on an eminence skirted by the Thames, and affords a beautiful view of the Oxford and Buckinghamshire hills, clothed with woods, and interspersed with numerous villas, belonging to the neighbouring gentlemen, which, with their parks and ornamented grounds, separated by the Thames seen in the distance gliding beneath the hills, fringed with the majestic oak or beech, forms one of the finest landscapes in England.

The park and pleasure grounds are extensive, but not open to the public without leave: this, however, is readily granted on application at the house, and those who have a taste for rural scenery will be highly gratified by viewing the various prospects afforded by the surrounding country, from this enchanting spot.

The village has some neat cottages in it, but though situated on a rising ground and offering every capability requisite to have rendered it one of the pleasantest in England, it is so irregularly built, and with such an apparent design to exclude every distant object however beautiful, that it might as well have been placed in the lowest and most confined situation.

Passing the bridge at this place, you enter Oxfordshire, and soon come to the turnpike road leading to Henley, distant about four miles. The road to this place is hilly, but affords several beautiful views of the Thames and the opposite hills of Berkshire. At a small distance from the road is Caversham

Park, the seat of Charles Marsack, esq. It formerly belonged to the Craven family, by one of whom it was alienated at the beginning of the last century to General Cadogan, the friend and companion of the great Marlborough in all his wars. At his death it descended to his brother Lord Cadogan, whose son, the late Lord Cadogan, sold it to the present possessor. After the unsuccessful attempt of Charles I. to relieve the garrison of Reading then besieged by the Earl of Essex, by forcing the passage of Caversham bridge, he retired to this place, where he passed the night, and the next day retreated with his troops to Nettlebed. At a subsequent period, when his Majesty was a prisoner to the army, he was suffered to reside here some time, and at the intercession of General Fairfax to the Parliament was permitted to see his children, at which time we are told in a letter to the Speaker signed by secretary Williamson, "here was a gallant Court, and his Majesty very *cheerful*, being attended by many brave gallants." The house was very much improved by the late possessor, and the gardens laid out in a superior style. The park, containing about five hundred acres, is situated at the back of the house, and surrounded by a ring fence; it is very well stocked with timber, particularly beech, oak, and chestnut, which being well adapted to the soil, have grown to an enormous size. One oak in particular, though short in the stem, has been valued at more than one hundred pounds, on account of its numerous branches being so peculiarly well formed to be converted into knees for ships of war of large dimensions.

There is a narrow valley runs thro' the middle of the park, along which the road is formed, but so shaded with trees that I always experience a chilling cold whenever I attempt to walk thro' it, at the same time that they deprive me of those distant views I so much admire. Perhaps I am somewhat singular in my taste, but I must confess this is not a favorite spot with me.

In the same neighbourhood, but in my opinion much better situated in point of prospect, is a little thatched cottage belonging to a Mr. Williams, not built in the grotesque stile of modern cottages, with stumps of trees stuck up like *pillars*, to represent houses of the poor which never *have any*

a narrow valley: Milestone Way, the spine footpath of Caversham Park Village, now follows the route of the former main drive to the big house.

a little thatched cottage: this is probably Farmcote, on Surley Row, where lived the custodian of the spring mentioned below. Man clearly disapproves of the fad for building 'cottages ornées'.

Mr. Williams: T E Williams senior, chemist, druggist and vet. He was evidently a friend of Man's, and tenant of the Castle Street house while Man was in the High Street.

such ornament; and green painted verandas, in appearance to keep off the rays of the sun from its inhabitants, who at the same time you are to suppose, from the style of the building, to spend their days in the open air, exposed to all their influence.

Unlike these, Mr. Williams' cottage remains exteriorly such as it always was, an unadorned thatched dwelling; the only difference is in the interior, which is fitted up in a neat but not a splendid manner, and furnished with every accommodation for a small family. There is a *simplex mundities* about it, that pleases at first sight, and grows on you the longer you stay. The only part I disapprove is the garden, as being too gaudy, and in every respect dissonant to the outward appearance of the dwelling to which it is annexed. I would have every part in unison; and as the house is to represent a poor man's residence, why should not the garden correspond with that idea? Over one of the windows is the following cento:

> This humble cottage boasts no foreign aid,
> No sculptur'd marble dome or high cascade:
> No splended poverty, no fawning fear,
> No well-bred hate, or servile grandeur here:
> Nature alone with mimic art contends,
> And every point of view a prospect lends,
> While pleasing objects useful thoughts suggest,
> The sense is ravish'd and the soul is blest.

I cannot give you a better idea of the distant objects seen from this delightful spot, than by transcribing the following lines I picked up in an old newspaper:

THE COTTAGE: most of these verses, undoubtedly by Man himself, are to be found in the *Anecdotes*. It is most unlikely that you could ever have seen all the places mentioned from Surley Row.

THE COTTAGE.

Now farewell Reading, with thy train
Of *puritanic tricks for gain,*
   Thy *praise* let others sing;
A nobler scene demands my lays,
Where Nature all her charms displays,
   In everlasting Spring.

This little Cottage all admire,
Its straw-clad roof and rustic fire,
   Its artless rooms and stairs,
Its pleasant garden with its fruit,
Which none but genial climates suit,
   Without the gard'ner's cares.

Enraptur'd! here I'll take my stand,
And view the sweet surrounding land,
   Where spires on spires arise;
The leafy wood or dusky hill,
Th'astonish'd sight with wonder fill,
   And bound the distant skies.

First Caversham with all its charms,
Of rural cottages and farms,
   Appears below the hill;
Its church where Barry's powers prevail,
Its pleasant meads and lovely vale,
   Its villas and its mill.

Old Thames next strikes the ravish'd eye,
Through all the meads meand'ring by
   In solemn pace profound;

And Reading stands full in my view,
Where mammon cherishes a few,
  And leaves the rest *a-ground*.

Above the town see Kennet creep,
As though his waters were a-sleep,
  'Till torrents drown the strand;
When rushing furious o'er his sides,
He spreads around his wat'ry tides,
  And seas o'erwhelm the land.

As far as distant sight can ken,
Fair Cottington surmounts the fen,
  Where scatter'd hamlets lie;
'Till hills on hills are seen to rise,
Majestic mounting to the skies,
  And intercept the eye.

Cottington: Cottington's Hill is 15 miles away in Hampshire, near Watership Down.

I see beside the left-hand road
The noble Blandford's sweet abode,
  His park with lofty trees;
The gentle stream that flows through all,
Affords a pleasing water-fall,
  And wavers with the breeze.

Blandford's: Whiteknights Park, now the University campus.

How faint are human pow'rs to trace,
The glowing magic of thy face,
  O Woodley! beauteous spot!
No wonder Nature owns his sway,
Whom jarring Senators obey*—
  Since here a *home* she's got.

* Mr. Addington, now Lord Sidmouth

Surmounting all I see the Holt:
The skipping lamb, the sheep, the colt,
   Fill all the heathy space;
Bill-Hill appears romantic, rude,
Surrounded by the neighb'ring wood,
   Within the royal chace.

Still to the left I stretch my sight,
Where Ruscomb's charms the soul delight,
   The seat of Baron Eyre;
No more the bench shall hear him plead,
The *cause* of *innocence* or *need*,
   With more than Roman fire.

Nor shall my muse refuse to sing
The raptures Sonning's Woodlands bring,
Where Nature deigns to live;
There Palmer's mansion stands confest,
With ev'ry *rural image* drest,
Assistant arts can give.

Last in the beauteous scene's display'd
The seat of royalty and trade,
Where George our Sov'reign dwells,
Whose patriot breast oft' swells with grief
To see the subject want relief,
Whose sorrows *Patience* tells.

Then here I'll fix my last abode,
Where ev'ry path with flowers is strow'd,
And pass a life serene;
Nor covet honors, titles, dress,

No cares can e'er my soul oppress,
While bless'd with such a scene.

And thou, sweet Poesy, I pray,
Be thou my guest from day to day,
  So time shall quickly fly;
And with thee bring the jocund Muse,
Thy company she'll not refuse, –
Then come sweet Poesy.

chalybeate spring: Discovered in 1803 in the grounds of Springfield, the big white house on Surley Row. In 1805 you could buy a quarterly season ticket to Caversham Spa for 10s 6d, or take the water away at 6d a gallon. Williams installed a pump, erected a gothic shelter, and planned a botanic garden. The cottage was advertised to let in 1818 'with the gardens, Advantages and Profits that may arise from the same'.

At a small distance from the house is a physic garden, belonging to the same gentleman, where a chalybeate spring has lately been discovered, which, from the great benefit several persons have already received by drinking the waters, promises to be of great service in the cure of various diseases. It is said to exceed in strength and efficacy every other chalybeate yet known.

"On analysis, it is found to be highly saturated with iron, held in solution by carbonic acid gas. A sulphureous gas is also distinguishable in it by the smell, but this is not sufficiently strong to give it a decided character. On being infused on vegetable astringents, such as galls or tea, the liquor becomes black like ink. Exposed to the air for a short time, it looses its brilliancy, and in a few hours becomes muddy, most probably from the escape of the carbonic acid gas. In about two days it deposits all the iron as the tests no longer detect it in the water. A residuum weighing 32 grains was obtained from one gallon of the water, the greater part whereof seemed to be an oxyd of iron." *

Near the spring are several lodging houses, whither it has long been the practice of the medical gentlemen here to send their invalid patients, for the benefit of the air, which they consider much purer than that in the smoky atmosphere of Reading: whether this opinion be founded in justice or not, I do not pretend to determine; but certain it is, that either from the salutary quality of the spring, or the air, many persons

---

* Rev. T. E. Williams' observations on the virtues of the chalybeate.

have received very great benefit by residing here; and nothing seems wanting but the sanction of some persons in high rank to render it in the *opinion of the public* the *most salubrious*, as it is confessed to be the most pleasant, spot in the county.

Beyond this charming spot, towards the west is Grove Park, the seat and residence of Mrs. Fell, combining in the house and grounds about it, every thing calculated to give a zest to a country residence.

There are many very pleasant rides in this parish; but one in particular struck me more than any I had ever seen: this is a bridle road leading along the brow of a hill to Mapledurham, where is a seat belonging to Michael Blount, esq. At the bottom of the hill on the right, the Thames is seen meandring through the vale below, spotted with islands and eyots as far as the eye can reach, sometimes disappearing, and again opening to the eye, but shorn by the distance, of all its majesty. On the left, Caversham-bridge appears like a distant ruin, but apparently connected with the town of Reading which is seen on the eastern extremity of a circular ridge of hills enclosing the spectator as in an amphitheatre.

like a distant ruin: it appeared ruinous because the Oxfordshire half was properly made of stone, while Reading could only afford a flimsy wooden structure. It was rebuilt in iron in 1869 and in concrete in 1926.

About a mile from Mapledurham is Hardwick House, the seat of P.L. Powis, esq. possessing no recommendation either in the style or elegance of the building to attract the notice of the traveller, but the woods about it will afford him some delightful rides, as well as the open country, the high road skirting the banks of the Thames all the way to Whitchurch, where are several gentlemen's seats, among these there is one lately erected by Samuel Gardiner, esq. on an eminence gently rising from the banks of the river, and commanding an

erected by Samuel Gardiner: Coombe Lodge.

extensive view on the East and West sides, but that on the South, which is in front of the house, is too much confined by the hills on the opposite side the river, whose tops being covered with woods confine the view from the house to a very short distance.

The bridge over the Thames at this place leads to the pleasant village of Pangbourn, through which passes the turnpike road to Oxford, deservedly admired by travellers for the variety and beauty of its scenery 'till you leave the county at Shillingford bridge.

Turning to the left at the distance of two miles, you come to Englefield, another village highly deserving your attention. Richard Benyon, esq. is lord of the manor: it formerly belonged to the Paulets, who appear to have taken up their residence here after the siege and destruction of Basing-house in the civil war in the reign of Charles I. The house is an elegant structure situated at the foot of a hill, which advances so near the leaded platform on the top, that, according to the tradition of the place, a coach and four was once driven from it round the battlements. The grounds about it are laid out in a good style, and are much increased in effect by a large piece of water in the park, which, with its islands stocked with water fowl of various descriptions, gives additional relief to the scenery.

Englefield: the house, first built in about 1600, was remodelled before 1779, and altered four times in the 19th century.

You may return to Reading, by the Bath Road, a pleasant ride of about five miles. In your way you pass the seat of John Blagrave, esq. at Tilehurst, and further on Prospect-hill, the residence of J. E. Liebenrood, esq. situated on the summit of a steep hill, from whence you have a most extensive view of the surrounding country, but the situation is too exposed to

seat of John Blagrave: Calcot House, built after 1759.

Prospect-hill: The 1800 Mansion House in Prospect Park, now a pub.

make it desirable.—I conceive that any prospect however picturesque, must, by custom, loose all its effect; it may charm from its novelty, but the eye tires by continually contemplating the same objects.

At the distance of something more than one mile, on the South side of the town, is White-knights, the seat of the Most Noble the Marquis of Blandford. The house was built by the late Sir H. Englefield, whose agricultural pursuits induced him to lay out the grounds about it as a *ferme ornée*, the general features of which it still retains, except in the park and gardens, which have been much improved by the present possessor, both by planting and ornamental buildings, but particularly by the number and variety of exotic plants, covering several acres of ground, and divided into distinct compartments according to the countries from whence they came, as the American, South Sea, Botany Bay, &c. gardens; but these, on account of the great value justly attached to them, cannot be seen by strangers without permission of the Marquis—however the park is at all times open to the public, who claim a prescriptive right of passing through it unmolested; this is not only a great convenience to those who have occasion to go that way, but a high gratification to every one who can enjoy the luxuries of rural scenery, presented in one of the most charming spots in England.

At a short distance from White-knights is the pleasant seat of E. Golding, esq. This is a large brick building, having nothing particular to recommend it except the grounds about it, which if not laid out in so ornamental a style as the last, are, I believe, more extensive, and better calculated to correspond with the surrounding scenery.

Marquis of Blandford: soon after this was written, it became clear that the profligate gardener and bibliophile was heading inexorably towards bankruptcy.

seat of E. Golding: Edward Golding (1746–1818) was a nabob; he spent fifteen years amassing a fortune in India, returning to Maiden Erlegh in 1779.

There are many other gentlemen's seats in this neighbourhood, as well as pleasant rides and rural walks, which the limits of a letter will not permit me to describe, but will amply repay the trouble of a personal visit whenever you shall have the opportunity of stopping any time here.

I have enclosed a few *Anecdotes* for your amusement, that owed their origin to this place, just as I have found them; some I have collected by reading, and others have been told me by persons resident here, but I do not take upon me to guarantee the truth of either, though I believe many of them to be authentic.—One of these however I cannot help inserting here, as combining an instance of that independent spirit so remarkable in our brave seamen, but which unluckily, for want of reflection, often turns to their own injury.

Anecdotes: these were never published, but do survive: see introduction.

One of these brave fellows, whom I shall call Boots, as honest a tar as ever spliced a rope, or handled a main-sail, and who, if report says true, could even box the compass, has resided here some years. As seamen however are generally exposed to more hardships than fall to the share of other persons, so it happened to poor Boots, for being on the watch on board his ship one very severe night, in the Baltic, his toes were so frozen as to render him incapable of following his calling any longer. On being discharged from his ship, he came to this place and commenced the industrious if not *lucrative* profession of a shoe-black, in which he was encouraged by most of the gentlemen and tradesmen here, who, it must be acknowledged, are never wanting in relieving the wants or encouraging the exertions of the industrious. One of his employers being unexpectedly called to London on the next day, and thinking it would be more convenient to our hero to

clean his boots that evening, than to be disturbed for that purpose at an early hour the next morning, sent his servant with
a request that the boots might be cleaned that night; unfortunately when the girl arrived Boots was just *turned into his
hammock*, and hearing the message, which was delivered in
rather a peremptory stile, he was so offended at the affront as
he conceived offered to his independence, that he positively

refused to clean them that night, telling her to take them back again, but this being also refused on her part, Boots quitted his hammock and huddling on his cloathes in a great rage, seized the boots and carried them back to his employer's himself. Exulting in what he had done, Boots hobbled home as fast as his crippled feet would carry him, and once more turned in; but his mind was so much disturbed for fear the boots should not be cleaned in time, that after passing a sleepless night, he arose at four o'clock, cleaned the boots and taking them in his hand to his employer, here, says he, is your honor's boots, I have taken them *into dock* and *careened* them I hope to your honor's liking, *but d—n me if I turn out of my berth before my watch for any man in England.*

I have now concluded my remarks on this town, and shall leave it to-morrow for Bath, where you may expect to hear from me soon, 'till when

I am, &c.
Reading, Sept. 5, 1809.

FINIS.

THE
Stranger in Reading,

IN

A SERIES OF LETTERS,

FROM

A TRAVELLER,

TO HIS

Friend in London.

Ridentem dicere verum, quid vetat?

In città da ciéchi beáto è chi ha un ócchio.

READING.

PRINTED BY SNARE AND MAN.
Sold by R. Snare, the other Booksellers in Reading,
and J. Richardson, Royal Exchange,
London.

1810.

The 1810 edition's title-page and frontispiece (showing 'Boots' – see p. 121)

as impossible for any one to *forget the situation* of his shop, as for the most cautious passenger to pass through this chaos without bringing away some *token* of the different articles the gentleman deals in.   On the same side the way, I met with an obstruction of a different kind : on my right hand was ranged a quantity of second-hand houshold furniture, and on my left was *a cellar window,* wide open, and extending nearly across the foot-path; to pass these, without danger, was impossible ; I therefore crossed over to my inn, took a hearty, and well-dressed, dinner, and then sat down to give you the above account of my peregrinations ; which, I fear, you are by this time heartily tired of.   I therefore conclude, with my best wishes.

Your's, &c.

Reading, ————

LETTER III.

To ——————

I Hinted in my last, at the broken and imperfect state of the pavement in this town ; whether the Commissoners are sleeping, or only want jogging, I know not ; but it seems to be high time they were roused, lest they fall into the *pits* they have left for others, or break their necks by tripping against the fragments of broken stones, in many places overtopping the level of the adjoining pavement several inches, in which state they are left day after day, a nuisance to passengers, without the least notice being taken of them, by those whose duty it is to guard the public from injury.

About the middle of the sixteenth century, the then existing Corporation

F 2

A typical spread showing Snare and Man's layout and typography in the 1810 edition

131

Nice new! Nice new!

Milk below!

The original Man illustrations – *Nice new* (see p. 37) and *Milk below* (see p. 38)